WHAT ARE THE BOOKS OF HOSEA–MICAH?

Kids' Guides to God's Word Series

What Are the Books of
HOSEA–MICAH?

Michael Whitworth

ISBN 978-1-971767-27-7

Published by Start2Finish
Bend, Oregon 97702
start2finish.org

Printed in the United States of America

30 29 28 27 26   1 2 3 4 5

CONTENTS

INTRODUCTION

Let's get something out of the way right up front: the word "minor" is misleading. When people hear "Minor Prophets," they assume it means "not that important." Minor league. Minor character. Minor detail. Skip it and move on to the good stuff.

But that's not what "minor" means here. These books aren't called minor because their messages are small. They're called minor because the books themselves are short. Some of the Minor Prophets are only a few pages long. Obadiah, the shortest, is just twenty-one verses. You could read it during a commercial break.

But short doesn't mean lightweight. These twelve small books, tucked between the Major Prophets and the New Testament, contain some of the most powerful, disturbing, beautiful, and important words in the entire Bible. A verse from Amos showed up in Martin Luther King Jr.'s most famous speech. A verse from Micah was chosen above every other religious text in the world to represent the idea of faith in the Library of Congress. A verse from Jonah was quoted by Jesus himself as a sign of his own death and resurrection. And a prophecy from Micah told the Magi exactly where to find the newborn King.

These are not minor books. They're short books with enormous things to say.

This volume covers the first six: Hosea, Joel, Amos, Obadiah, Jonah, and Micah. And together, they tell a story you need to hear.

WHERE WE ARE IN THE STORY

To understand the Minor Prophets, you need to know what happened before they showed up.

After God rescued Israel from Egypt, gave them his law, and brought them into the promised land, things went well for a while. Joshua led the conquest. The judges kept the nation alive through three centuries of chaos. Then came the kings: Saul, David, and Solomon. Under David and Solomon, Israel became a united, powerful kingdom. Solomon built the temple in Jerusalem. It looked like everything God had promised was finally coming together.

Then it fell apart.

After Solomon died, the kingdom split in two. The northern kingdom kept the name Israel, with its capital at Samaria. The southern kingdom was called Judah, with its capital at Jerusalem. The northern kings were, almost without exception, disasters. They set up rival worship centers, promoted idolatry, and led the people further and further from God. The southern kings were a mixed bag: some were faithful, some were terrible, and most were somewhere in between.

By the eighth century BC, both kingdoms were in serious trouble. The wealthy were exploiting the poor. The courts were corrupt. The priests were compromised. The worship centers were packed with people who loved religious rituals but ignored the God behind them. And on the horizon, the Assyrian Empire was growing stronger by the year, swallowing up smaller nations like a fire consuming dry grass.

This is the world the Minor Prophets stepped into. They didn't come with armies or political power. They came with words, and those words were from God.

WHAT YOU'RE ABOUT TO READ

Each of the six prophets in this volume has a distinct voice, a distinct setting, and a distinct message. But they all share a common thread: God is not silent when his people go wrong, and he is not finished when judgment falls.

Hosea is the prophet whose personal life became his message. God told him to marry a woman who would be unfaithful, and through that broken marriage, Hosea experienced firsthand what it felt like to love someone who kept walking away. His book is the most emotionally raw in the Old Testament. It's about a God who has every reason to give up on his people and refuses to do it.

Joel is the prophet of the locust plague. A devastating swarm strips the land bare, and Joel uses the crisis to warn of something even worse: the coming day of the Lord. But right in the middle of the destruction, Joel delivers one of the most hopeful promises in Scripture: God will pour out his Spirit on all people. That promise was fulfilled on the day of Pentecost in Acts 2, and it's still being fulfilled today.

Amos is the prophet of justice. A farmer from the southern kingdom who was sent to preach in the north, Amos took aim at the wealthy elite who lived in luxury while the poor were sold into slavery for the price of a pair of sandals. His most famous line, "Let justice roll on like a river," is as urgent now as it was twenty-eight centuries ago.

Obadiah is the prophet of the betrayed brother. His target is Edom, the nation descended from Esau, Jacob's twin. When Jerusalem fell, Edom stood by and watched, then looted the wreckage and handed fleeing survivors over to the enemy. Obadiah's message is short and sharp: what you did to your brother will be done to you.

Jonah is the prophet who ran. Told to preach to Nineveh, the capital of Israel's greatest enemy, Jonah boarded a ship heading the opposite direction. What followed is the most famous fish story in history. But the real point of the book isn't the fish. It's the question God asks at the end, a question about mercy that the prophet never answers and the reader is meant to wrestle with forever.

Micah is the prophet of the small town. From the village of Moresheth in the Judean foothills, he challenged the corruption of Jerusalem's leaders with a courage that came straight from the Spirit of God. He predicted that Jerusalem would be plowed like a field, that a ruler would come from tiny Bethlehem, and that what God really wants from his people is not thousands of sacrifices but three simple things: justice, mercy, and a humble walk with him.

WHY THIS MATTERS FOR YOU

You might be thinking that books written in the eighth century BC to people in the ancient Near East can't possibly have anything to say to your life. But here's the thing: the problems the prophets addressed haven't gone away.

People still exploit the vulnerable. Courts still fail the powerless. Religious people still go through the motions without letting their faith change how they treat others. Nations still rise and fall. And individuals still run from what God is calling them to do.

The Minor Prophets spoke to all of it. They spoke about injustice and called it what it was. They spoke about empty worship and tore off the mask. They spoke about God's judgment and didn't flinch. And they spoke about God's mercy—his stubborn, relentless, inexhaustible mercy—that outlasts every sin and every empire and every act of human rebellion.

These books also point to Jesus. Hosea's promise that God would raise his people "on the third day" echoes in the resurrection. Joel's promise of the Spirit poured out was fulfilled at Pentecost. Amos' vision of David's restored kingdom was quoted by James at the Jerusalem council. Jonah's three days in the fish became Jesus' sign of his own burial and rising. And Micah's prophecy about Bethlehem guided the Magi to the manger.

The Minor Prophets aren't an optional section of the Bible. They're the bridge between the Old Testament story and the New Testament fulfillment. Skip them, and you miss the setup. Read them, and the whole picture comes into focus.

BEFORE YOU START

These are real books written to real people about real problems. They're sometimes beautiful and sometimes brutal. They contain poetry that will take your breath away and judgments that will make you uncomfortable. They were written by men who had the courage to say what nobody wanted to hear, because the God who sent them cared too much to stay silent.

Six prophets. Six messages. One God who judges because he is just, restores because he is faithful, and forgives because he delights in mercy.

Turn the page.

1

A LOVE STORY NOBODY SAW COMING

Have you ever had a friend who kept letting you down? Not once, not twice, but over and over again. Maybe they promised to save you a seat and didn't. Maybe they talked about you behind your back, apologized, and then did it again a week later. Maybe they kept choosing other people over you, and every time you thought things were getting better, they went right back to the same old pattern.

Now imagine something harder. Imagine that you didn't just stay friends with that person. Imagine that God told you to. Imagine God saying, "I want you to keep loving them, even though they're going to hurt you. Not because they deserve it, but because I need to show the world what my love looks like."

That's the book of Hosea. And it starts with one of the most shocking commands God ever gave a prophet.

THE MAN AND THE MOMENT

Hosea was a prophet in the northern kingdom of Israel. He began preaching around 760 BC, during a time when Israel looked like it was doing great. The economy was strong. The borders were secure. King Jeroboam II had been on the throne for decades, and the nation was enjoying a level of wealth and comfort it hadn't seen in years.

But underneath the prosperity, everything was rotting. The people had drifted far from God. They still called themselves his people. They still showed up at their worship centers and went through the motions. But they had blended their worship of the Lord with the worship of a Canaanite god called Baal, a storm and fertility god that the surrounding nations credited with making crops grow and rain fall. Israelite farmers figured it couldn't hurt to worship Baal on the side, just in case. Some of them had gone so far that they couldn't tell the difference between the Lord and Baal anymore.

The worship of Baal wasn't just wrong theology. It was ugly. It involved rituals at hilltop shrines under sacred trees, sometimes including sexual acts as part of the worship. Incense was burned to Baal at altars scattered across the countryside. The people credited Baal for the grain, the wine, and the olive oil that God had actually given them. They took God's gifts and said "thank you" to someone else.

That's the world Hosea was called to confront. And the way God chose to deliver the message was unlike anything anyone had ever seen.

THE COMMAND THAT CHANGED EVERYTHING

God's first words to Hosea were staggering: "Go, marry a woman who will be unfaithful to you, and have children with her, because this land has been completely unfaithful to the Lord."

Let that sink in. God didn't tell Hosea to preach a sermon. He told him to marry someone who would break his heart. On purpose. Because God wanted Hosea to experience, in his own body and his own home, a fraction of what God himself felt every single day as he watched his people chase after other gods.

Hosea obeyed. He married a woman named Gomer. And what followed wasn't just a difficult marriage. It was a living picture of God's relationship with Israel, acted out in real time for everyone to see.

THREE CHILDREN, THREE WARNINGS

Gomer and Hosea had three children, and God gave each child a name that carried a message for the entire nation. If you've ever met someone with an unusual name and wondered about the story behind it, imagine meeting these kids. Their names were walking prophecies.

The first child, a son, was named Jezreel. That was the name of a valley where, a century earlier, a king named Jehu had carried out a brutal massacre to seize the throne. The bloodshed at Jezreel was supposed to purify Israel, but it only led to more violence, more corruption, more of the same. By naming his son Jezreel, Hosea was announcing that God hadn't forgotten that blood, and that judgment was coming for the royal house. In fact, it came within a few years. Jeroboam II's son was assassinated after only six months on the throne, and the kingdom spiraled into chaos.

The second child, a daughter, received a name that meant "Not Loved." God was saying through this child's name that he would no longer show his protective compassion to the northern kingdom. They had pushed his patience past the breaking point. He would still love Judah in the south, but Israel had run out of second chances.

The third child, another son, got the worst name of all: "Not My People." God was declaring that the covenant relationship was over. The bond that had defined Israel since the days of Moses, the promise that said "I will be your God, and you will be my people," was being formally dissolved. Israel had acted like they didn't belong to God, so God was making it official.

Imagine Hosea walking through town with these three children. Every time someone asked their names, the conversation became a sermon. "What's your daughter's name?" "Not Loved." "And your youngest?" "Not My People." No one could hear those names without asking why. And that was exactly the point.

A SUDDEN REVERSAL

But then, without any warning, the tone changes completely. Right after the devastating announcement that Israel is no longer God's people, God says this: "Yet the Israelites will be like the sand on the seashore, which cannot be measured or counted. In the place where it was said to them, 'You are not my people,' they will be called 'sons of the living God.'"

Every terrible name gets reversed. "Not Loved" becomes "Loved." "Not My People" becomes "My People." Even "Jezreel," which had meant scattering and slaughter, takes on its other meaning: "God plants." The God who scattered would one day sow his people back into their land.

This reversal is so sudden it's jarring. There's no transition, no explanation of how the nation gets from total rejection to total restoration. That's deliberate. Hosea wants you to feel the impossibility of it. Only God could bridge a gap that wide. Only grace that enormous could take people who deserved to be cast off and call them sons and daughters instead.

Centuries later, in the book of Romans, the apostle Paul quoted these exact verses to explain how people who had never been part of God's family, including non-Jewish believers, were being welcomed in. The promise Hosea made to broken Israel turned out to be big enough for the whole world.

THE CASE AGAINST THE UNFAITHFUL WIFE

Chapter 2 shifts from the children to the mother. Now God speaks as a husband whose wife has walked out on him. The language is the language of a courtroom. God is bringing charges.

The accusation is devastating. Israel, his bride, has chased after other lovers. She has credited them for the food on her table, the clothes on her back, the silver and gold in her treasury. "She said, 'I will go after my lovers, who give me my food and my water, my wool and my linen, my oil and my drink.'" But she was wrong. It was God who had provided all of it. She took his gifts and offered them to Baal.

So God announces what he will do. He will block her path. He will take back the grain and the wine. He will put an end to the festivals and celebrations she loved. He will strip away everything she thought her other lovers had given her, until she has nothing left and nowhere to turn.

It sounds harsh. But pay attention to what God is doing. He isn't destroying her out of spite. He is removing every distraction, every false source of comfort, every counterfeit love, so that she will finally come to her senses and say, "I will go back to my husband as at first, for then I was better off than now."

God's discipline has a destination. He isn't trying to crush Israel. He is trying to bring her home.

THE WILDERNESS AND THE WEDDING

Then comes one of the most beautiful passages in the entire Old Testament. God says, "I am now going to allure her; I will lead her into the wilderness and speak tenderly to her."

The wilderness. That's where God first brought Israel after rescuing her from Egypt. That's where she depended on him for everything: food, water, direction. Before the distractions of Canaan, before the temptations of Baal worship, before everything went sideways, there was the wilderness, and in that wilderness, Israel followed God closely.

God wants to start over. He wants to take his people back to the place where the relationship was simple and real. And what he promises next sounds like wedding vows: "I will betroth you to me forever. I will betroth you in righteousness and justice, in love and compassion. I will betroth you in faithfulness, and you will acknowledge the Lord."

Three times he says "I will betroth you." Each time the promise gets richer. God is offering not just forgiveness, but a completely renewed relationship built on his own character. The righteousness, the justice, the love, the compassion, the faithfulness that Israel never managed to produce on her own, God would bring as his gift to the marriage.

And the chapter ends with the children's names reversed one final time. God will plant his people in the land. He will show love to the one called "Not Loved." He will say to "Not My People," "You are my people." And they will answer, "You are my God."

BUYING HER BACK

Chapter 3 is short and quiet, but it might be the most powerful part of the whole story. God speaks to Hosea again: "Go, show your love to your wife again, even though she is loved by another and is unfaithful. Love her as the Lord loves the Israelites, though they turn to other gods."

Gomer had left. She had returned to her old life. And now she had sunk so low that Hosea had to buy her back, paying fifteen pieces of silver and some barley. The price was roughly what you'd pay to free a slave. The woman who had been Hosea's wife was now someone else's property, and Hosea had to scrape together the money to bring her home.

He didn't yell at her. He didn't lecture her. He just told her, "You are to live with me for many days. You will not be unfaithful, and I will live the same way with you." It was a period of healing, of rebuilding what had been destroyed, of learning to trust again.

Then Hosea explains what this means: Israel would go through a long period without a king, without a government of their own, without the familiar rituals they had relied on. It would feel like exile, and it would be. But afterward, God's people would return. They would seek the Lord their God. And they would come trembling to his goodness.

That's the pattern of the whole book. Sin, consequence, and then grace so outrageous it takes your breath away. A husband who should have given up but didn't. A God who had every reason to walk away but chose instead to pay the price and bring his people home.

WHAT THIS MEANS FOR US

First, God's love is not based on our performance. Gomer didn't deserve to be loved. Israel didn't deserve to be rescued. And yet God said, "Love her as I love them." His love isn't a reward for good behavior. It's a gift given to people who have done nothing to earn it. If you've ever felt like you're too far gone for God to care about you, this story says otherwise.

Second, sin is more serious than we think. Hosea doesn't describe Israel's unfaithfulness as a minor mistake or a harmless phase. He compares it to adultery, to the betrayal of the deepest relationship a person can have. When we treat God as optional—when we give the credit for our blessings to anything other than him, when we go through the motions of faith while chasing after other things—we are doing exactly what Israel did. And it matters.

Third, God's discipline is always aimed at restoration. The blocked paths, the failed harvests, the stripped-away blessings of chapter 2 weren't random punishments. They were a carefully designed plan to remove every false comfort until Israel had no choice but to look up and see the God who had been there all along. If your life feels like a wilderness right now, it's worth asking whether God might be clearing away distractions so you can hear his voice again.

Fourth, the gospel is already here. A God who pays the price to buy back someone who has betrayed him. A husband who absorbs the cost of his wife's unfaithfulness and offers her a fresh start. A love that says "you are my people" to those who had been told "you are not my people." If that doesn't sound like the story of Jesus, read it again.

TALKING POINTS

1. **God told Hosea to marry someone who would be unfaithful, specifically so that Hosea could understand how God felt about Israel.** What does this tell you about how personally God takes our relationship with him? Why do you think he wanted a prophet to feel that pain firsthand?

2. **The three children's names were living messages of judgment.** What would it have been like for Hosea's neighbors to hear those names every day? Why do you think God chose such a public and personal way to deliver his warning?

3. **God says Israel credited Baal for the grain, wine, and oil that God had actually provided.** What are some things people today credit for their success or happiness instead of acknowledging God? Why is it so easy to forget where good things really come from?

4. **In chapter 3, Hosea had to buy Gomer back, paying the price to redeem her from slavery.** How does this connect to what Jesus did for us? What does it mean to be "bought back" by someone who loves you?

5. God promised to lead Israel into the wilderness and "speak tenderly to her." Why would the wilderness, of all places, be where God wanted to restore the relationship? Have you ever gone through a hard season that ended up bringing you closer to God?

The marriage story of Hosea and Gomer is over. But the message it carried is just getting started. For the next seven chapters, God will lay out his full case against Israel, naming their sins with brutal honesty and showing exactly how far they have fallen from the people he called them to be. The charges are about to get specific.

Turn the page.

2

THE CHARGES

In Robert Louis Stevenson's *Treasure Island*, Long John Silver is the most likable man on the ship. He's warm, generous, and full of good stories. Young Jim Hawkins trusts him completely. Silver cooks for the crew. He looks out for the boy. He seems like exactly the kind of person you'd want on your side.

Then Jim crawls into an apple barrel one night, and everything changes. Hiding among the barrels, he overhears Silver laying out his real plan to the other sailors. Silver is a pirate. He's been planning a mutiny from the moment he stepped on board. Every friendly word, every warm smile, every act of kindness was a mask. The man Jim trusted most was the most dangerous person on the ship.

That scene, the moment the mask comes off, is what Hosea 4–10 feels like. For years, Israel looked like a faithful nation. The worship centers were packed. The sacrifices were flowing. The festivals were celebrated on schedule. But God could see what was hiding behind the religious performance, and in these chapters, he pulls back the curtain. What he reveals underneath is devastating.

Hosea 4–10 is God's full indictment. The love story of chapters 1–3 has been told. Now comes the evidence. And it is damning.

GOD TAKES THE STAND

Chapter 4 opens like a courtroom scene. God has a formal charge to bring against the people of Israel, and he lays it out in three short phrases: there is no faithfulness in the land, no love, and no knowledge of God.

Those three things were supposed to define Israel. Faithfulness meant keeping your word, being honest, being the kind of person others could count on. Love meant the deep, loyal commitment that people in a covenant relationship owed each other, the kind of love Hosea talked about in the opening chapters. And knowledge of God didn't just mean knowing facts about him. It meant knowing him personally, the way you know a parent or a close friend, and letting that relationship shape how you live.

All three were gone. And in their place? Cursing, lying, murder, theft, and adultery. The Ten Commandments weren't just being broken. They were being shattered, one after another, and nobody seemed to care. The violence had gotten so bad that, as Hosea put it, "bloodshed follows bloodshed." The whole nation was unraveling.

And the consequences weren't limited to human society. The land itself was suffering. The animals were dying. The fish were disappearing. When a nation abandons its relationship with the God who made everything, the damage ripples outward into creation itself. Israel's moral collapse was becoming an ecological one.

THE PRIESTS WHO FORGOT

If you're wondering how things got this bad, Hosea has an answer. He turns from the general population to the people who were supposed to be leading them: the priests.

In Israel, priests weren't just the people who handled sacrifices at the altar. They were teachers. They were responsible for passing on God's law to the people, for helping ordinary Israelites understand who God was and what he expected of them. They were the bridge between God and his people.

And they had completely failed.

"My people are destroyed for lack of knowledge," God says through Hosea. That's one of the most quoted lines in the entire book, and it's aimed squarely at the priests. The people didn't know God's law because the priests had stopped teaching it. Worse than that, the priests had "rejected knowledge" on purpose. They had decided it wasn't worth the trouble. They had traded their God-given calling for personal profit, because more sin meant more sin offerings, and more offerings meant more meat on the priests' tables. They were literally feeding off the people's guilt.

"Like people, like priest," God says. It's a grim proverb. The priests had sunk to the level of the people, and the people had sunk because the priests let them. Everyone was dragging everyone else down, and nobody was pulling anyone up.

The corruption went deep. People were consulting wooden idols for guidance and using divination sticks to make decisions, the kind of superstitious nonsense that belonged to the nations around them, not to the people of the living God. They were sacrificing on hilltops under oak trees and burning incense to Baal. The worship of the true God and the worship of false gods had become so tangled together that most Israelites couldn't tell the difference anymore.

Hosea even invents a mocking nickname for Bethel, one of Israel's main worship centers. Instead of calling it "House of God," which is what Bethel means, he calls it "House of Wickedness." The place where people went to worship had become the place where they sinned the most.

LOVE LIKE MORNING FOG

There's a brief moment near the beginning of chapter 6 where things seem to brighten. A voice rings out: "Come, let us return to the Lord. He has torn us to pieces but he will heal us; he has injured us but he will bind up our wounds. After two days he will revive us; on the third day he will restore us, that we may live in his presence. Let us press on to know the Lord."

Beautiful words. The kind of words you'd hope to hear from a people who had finally come to their senses. But God isn't fooled. He knows the difference between genuine repentance and a momentary burst of religious feeling. And his response cuts to the bone:

"What shall I do with you? Your love is like the morning mist, like the early dew that disappears."

Think about that image. Morning mist looks beautiful when the sun first rises. It covers the fields and makes everything look soft and promising. But give it an hour, and it's gone. There's nothing left. It vanished the moment the heat arrived.

That was Israel's devotion to God. Intense for a moment, gone by lunchtime. They could say all the right words. They could show up at the temple with armloads of sacrifices. But their hearts weren't in it. The commitment never lasted.

This is where God delivers one of the most important lines in the entire Old Testament: "I desire mercy, not sacrifice, and acknowledgment of God rather than burnt offerings." Jesus quoted this verse twice during his ministry. It's that important. God isn't interested in religious performances. He never has been. What he wants is a real relationship: loyal love and genuine knowledge of him. Everything else is just noise.

A KINGDOM COMING APART

Chapters 6–7 pull back the curtain on Israel's political chaos. And chaos is the right word for it. After King Jeroboam II died in 753 BC, the northern kingdom went through six kings in roughly thirty years. Most of them came to power by assassinating the king before them. The throne wasn't inherited; it was stolen, over and over again.

Hosea describes this with a vivid image. He compares Israel to an oven that a baker has stoked hot and then walked away from. The fire keeps burning while the dough rises, and by the time anyone checks, the heat has consumed everything. The political plotters in Israel were like that oven: burning with ambition, fueled by alcohol and scheming, destroying one king after another in their quest for power. "All their kings fall," Hosea observes, "and none of them calls on me." Not one of these rulers thought to ask God what he wanted. They were too busy grabbing power to notice they were tearing the country apart.

But the political problems weren't just domestic. Israel was also making terrible decisions on the international stage.

Caught between two superpowers—Egypt to the south and Assyria to the east—Israel's leaders kept flip-flopping between them. One king would pay tribute to Assyria. The next would send olive oil to Egypt, trying to buy an alliance. Then they'd switch back to Assyria when things got desperate.

Hosea has a devastating image for this: "Ephraim is like a dove, easily deceived and senseless, calling to Egypt, going to Assyria." A dove is a bird that's easy to trap. You scatter some bait and it walks right in. That was Israel, walking into one trap after another, too foolish to see the net closing around them.

He has another image too. Israel, he says, is like a flat cake that hasn't been turned over. One side is burnt, the other side is raw dough. It's a picture of something half-done, something ruined by neglect. Israel's attempts to play both sides of the international game left them burned on one side and useless on the other. They were, to use a phrase we still use today, completely half-baked.

And here's the saddest part: "Gray hairs are sprinkled on him, but he does not notice." Israel was aging, weakening, declining, and the nation didn't even realize it. Like someone who doesn't notice they're getting sick until it's too late, Israel was dying and couldn't see the symptoms.

SOWING THE WIND

Chapter 8 opens with an alarm. "Put the trumpet to your lips! An eagle is over the house of the Lord." Danger was coming. The Assyrian army, the most terrifying military force in the ancient world, was circling like a bird of prey.

Israel cried out to God: "Our God, we acknowledge you!" But God wasn't buying it. Their actions told a different story. They set up kings without God's approval. They made idols of silver and gold. They worshiped a golden calf at their shrine, the same kind of idol that had gotten their ancestors in trouble centuries earlier when they made one at the foot of Mount Sinai. "A metalworker has made it," God says with cutting simplicity. "It is not God." A thing made by human hands in a human workshop cannot save anyone. It will be smashed to pieces.

Then comes one of the most famous lines in the book: "They sow the wind and reap the whirlwind."

It's a farming image, and Hosea's audience would have understood it instantly. When you plant seeds, you expect to harvest something bigger than what you planted. A single kernel of wheat produces a stalk with dozens of kernels. That's how farming works. But Hosea flips it into a warning. Israel has been planting wind, which is nothing. And what they will harvest is a whirlwind, which is destruction. Their empty worship, their foolish alliances, their corrupt politics, all of it was planting nothing of value. And nothing of value was going to come back to them. Only something far worse than what they started with.

The chapter ends with a pointed reminder: "Israel has forgotten his Maker and built palaces; Judah has fortified many towns. But I will send fire on their cities that will consume their fortresses." Palaces and fortresses look impressive. They make people feel safe. But when you've forgotten the God who actually protects you, all the stone walls in the world won't save you.

THE HARVEST ARRIVES

Chapters 9–10 describe what happens when the bill comes due. The festivals will end. The worship centers will be destroyed. The golden calf that Israel cherished will be carried off to Assyria as plunder. The king will be swept away. The nation will become "wanderers among the nations," exiled from their homeland, scattered across the empire of the very power they had tried to play diplomatic games with.

Hosea reaches back into Israel's history to show that this pattern of rebellion is nothing new. He points to Baal Peor, where the Israelites had committed idolatry during the wilderness wanderings. He points to Gibeah, where an act of horrific violence had nearly wiped out an entire tribe during the time of the judges. Israel's current sins aren't an aberration. They are the latest chapter in a long story of choosing the wrong path.

But even in the middle of all this darkness, Hosea leaves a door open. "Sow righteousness for yourselves," he urges. "Reap the fruit of unfailing love, and break up your unplowed ground; for it is time to seek the Lord, until he comes and showers his righteousness on you."

The farming language is back, but this time it's hopeful. There is still time to plant something real. There is still time to seek God. The field isn't ruined beyond recovery, not yet. But the window is closing, and if the people don't act, the whirlwind will come.

WHAT THIS MEANS FOR US

First, what you don't know can destroy you. Israel's collapse didn't start with dramatic acts of rebellion. It started with ignorance, with priests who stopped teaching and people who stopped learning. The same thing can happen to us. If you don't know what God says, you won't know when you've drifted away from him. Spiritual ignorance isn't harmless. It's the first step toward everything else that goes wrong.

Second, religious activity is not the same as a real relationship with God. Israel offered sacrifices every day. They showed up at the temple. They celebrated the festivals. And God said, "I desire mercy, not sacrifice." You can go to church every Sunday, read your Bible every morning, and still miss the point entirely if your heart isn't actually turned toward God and toward loving the people around you. God sees through the performance. He always has.

Third, half-hearted commitment leads nowhere good. Israel's love was like morning mist. Intense for a moment, gone by noon. And their political strategy was like an unturned cake: burned on one side, raw on the other. Half-measures don't work in your relationship with God any more than they work in friendships. Either you're all in, or you're drifting.

Fourth, what you plant is what you harvest. This is one of the Bible's most consistent principles, and Hosea states it as clearly as anyone. If you plant nothing of value, you won't harvest anything of value. If you invest your time and energy in things that don't matter, don't be surprised when the return is empty. But the flip side is also true: plant righteousness, and you will reap love. Seek God, and he will come.

TALKING POINTS

1. **God's first charge against Israel was that there was "no faithfulness, no love, and no knowledge of God in the land."**

Which of those three do you think is most lacking in the world today? Which one do you most need to grow in personally?

2. **The priests were supposed to teach God's law but stopped doing it.** What happens to a community when its spiritual leaders stop taking their responsibilities seriously? Who are the people in your life who help you understand God, and what would happen if they stopped?

3. **God said Israel's love was "like the morning mist."** Have you ever felt really fired up about something, like your faith, a new habit, or a goal, and then lost that motivation quickly? What makes commitment last beyond the initial excitement?

4. **Israel kept going back and forth between Egypt and Assyria, trying to find security in political alliances instead of trusting God.** What are some things people today rely on for security instead of God? Why is it so tempting to look for safety in things we can see and control?

5. **Hosea told the people to "sow righteousness" and "seek the Lord."** What does it look like, practically, for someone your age to plant righteousness in everyday life? What kind of harvest do you think it produces?

The charges have been read. The evidence is overwhelming. Israel stands guilty of abandoning the God who loved them, ignoring the leaders who should have guided them, and chasing after every false promise the world dangled in front of them. But God isn't finished speaking. In the final chapters of Hosea, the tone is about to shift one more time, and what comes next will break your heart.

Turn the page.

3

THE HEART OF GOD

In Charles Dickens' *Oliver Twist*, a young orphan is pulled into the criminal underworld of London. Fagin and his gang of thieves take Oliver in, put stolen goods in his hands, and drag him deeper and deeper into a life that is destroying him. Oliver doesn't fully understand what's happening to him. He's a child, surrounded by people who are using him, and escape seems impossible.

But there are people on the outside who love him: Mr. Brownlow and Rose Maylie. They don't give up. When Oliver disappears into the streets, they search for him. When Fagin's gang recaptures him, they fight to get him back. No matter how lost Oliver seems, no matter how deep into the criminal world he's dragged, the people who love him refuse to let go. They pursue him until he's home.

The final chapters of Hosea are that kind of story. After several chapters of charges, evidence, and verdict, after every possible indictment has been laid at Israel's feet, the tone shifts. God stops prosecuting. He starts remembering. He remembers what it was like when Israel was young, when the relationship was new, when he held their hand and taught them to walk. And what comes pouring out is not more anger but something far more painful: the anguish of a parent watching a child throw everything away.

These chapters contain some of the most emotionally raw passages in the entire Bible. If you want to know what God feels when his people walk away from him, this is where you look.

WHEN ISRAEL WAS A CHILD

Chapter 11 opens with a shift that catches you off guard. After chapters of courtroom language and lists of crimes, God suddenly sounds like a father looking through old photographs.

"When Israel was a child, I loved him, and out of Egypt I called my son." That single sentence reaches all the way back to the exodus, to the moment when God rescued a nation of slaves from the most powerful empire on earth. Israel was young then, completely dependent, and God loved them. He chose them. He called them out of bondage and made them his own.

Then comes an image so tender it almost hurts to read: "It was I who taught Ephraim to walk, taking them by the arms." Picture a parent crouching down, holding a toddler's hands, watching them take those wobbly first steps. That's how God describes what he did for Israel. He didn't just issue commands from a distance. He got down on their level. He held them up. He guided their feet.

"I led them with cords of human kindness, with ties of love. To them I was like one who lifts a little child to the cheek, and I bent down to feed them."

Every image here is physical, intimate, personal. Lifting a child to your cheek. Bending down to put food in their mouth. This is not the language of a king addressing subjects. This is the language of a parent who adores their child. And that's exactly the point. Before we hear what went wrong, God wants us to know what it cost him. He wants us to understand that the people who betrayed him were not strangers. They were his kids.

THE CHILD WHO WALKED AWAY

But the more God called, the further Israel ran. "They sacrificed to the Baals and they burned incense to images." The child who had been carried in God's arms grew up and chose other gods. The nation that had been taught to walk used its legs to walk away.

God had healed them, but they didn't realize who was doing the healing. He had fed them, but they gave the credit to someone else. The same tragic pattern from the earlier chapters appears again: Israel receiving God's love with one hand and reaching for idols with the other.

Now the consequences arrive. Because they refused to return to God, the sword would rage through their cities. Assyria would swallow them. Their own plans, the clever political strategies and religious compromises they had relied on, would devour them from the inside. Israel had chosen its path, and the path led to destruction.

This is where the chapter could have ended. Guilty verdict. Sentence carried out. Case closed.

But God isn't finished.

HOW CAN I GIVE YOU UP?

What comes next is unlike anything else in the Old Testament. God is not speaking to Israel. He is speaking to himself. And what he says reveals a war raging inside the heart of God between justice and love:

"How can I give you up, Ephraim? How can I hand you over, Israel? How can I treat you like Admah? How can I make you like Zeboiim?"

Admah and Zeboiim were cities destroyed alongside Sodom and Gomorrah, wiped off the face of the earth for their wickedness. God is asking himself: Can I really do that to my own people? Can I destroy them the way I destroyed those cities? They deserve it. The evidence is overwhelming. The verdict is clear.

And then: "My heart is changed within me; all my compassion is aroused. I will not carry out my fierce anger, nor will I devastate Ephraim again. For I am God, and not a man, the Holy One among you. I will not come against you in fury."

This is one of the most staggering statements in the Bible. God's reason for showing mercy is not that Israel has earned it. They haven't. His reason is that he is God and not a human being. A human being in God's position would have walked away long ago. A human husband, betrayed as thoroughly as God has been betrayed, would have been done with it. A human father, watching a child reject everything he offered, would eventually stop trying.

But God is not human. His love is not like ours. It doesn't run out. It doesn't reach a limit and give up. It keeps going when any reasonable person would have quit, because the one doing the loving is not a reasonable person. He is God.

The chapter ends with a promise: God will roar like a lion, not against his people this time but on their behalf, and his children will come trembling from the west, from Egypt, from Assyria. He will settle them in their homes again. The exile will not be the end of the story.

LOOKING BACKWARD

Chapter 12 takes a step back and looks at Israel's history through the lens of Jacob, the patriarch whose very name became the name of the nation. Jacob had been a schemer from birth, grasping his brother's heel in the womb, tricking his father for a blessing, wrestling with God at the river Jabbok. But for all his scheming, Jacob eventually came face to face with God and was changed.

Hosea's point is that Israel has inherited Jacob's worst traits without learning Jacob's most important lesson. They are schemers. Their merchants use dishonest scales. Their diplomats make worthless treaties with Assyria and Egypt. They cheat and deceive and then say, "But look how rich we are! No one can find any sin in us."

God isn't fooled. He reminds them that he is the same God who brought them out of Egypt through a prophet, who cared for them through Moses in the wilderness. He has sent prophets and visions and warnings, generation after generation. Israel's problem isn't that they haven't been told. It's that they refuse to listen.

THE LION, THE LEOPARD, AND THE GRAVE

Chapter 13 is fierce. God describes himself as a lion, a leopard, a bear robbed of her cubs. These are not comforting images. They are images of raw, dangerous power directed at a people who have exhausted every opportunity to turn back. The golden calf that Israel worshiped, the one craftsmen built with their own hands, will be smashed to pieces. The king Israel trusted will be swept away. The nation's wealth, stored up in treasuries and granaries, will be plundered when the east wind of Assyria comes blowing across the land.

The chapter contains some of the most devastating prophecy in the book. The horrors of war are described in terms that make you flinch. Hosea is not softening the picture. He wants Israel to feel the weight of what is coming, to understand that these are not empty threats.

But buried in the middle of this darkness is a line that changes everything. "I will deliver this people from the power of the grave; I will redeem them from death. Where, O death, are your plagues? Where, O grave, is your destruction?"

In context, these words may carry the sting of a threat: God summoning death itself against a rebellious nation. But centuries later, the apostle Paul picked up this verse and turned it into a shout of victory. In his letter to the church at Corinth, Paul quoted these words after declaring that Jesus had conquered death through his resurrection. "Where, O death, is your victory? Where, O death, is your sting?" What began as a dark prophecy in Hosea became one of the most triumphant lines in the New Testament. The same God who warned of death's power over Israel also had the power to defeat death forever.

COME HOME

And then, after everything, comes chapter 14. It is the shortest chapter in the book, and it is beautiful.

"Return, O Israel, to the Lord your God. Your sins have been your downfall! Take words with you and return to the Lord. Say to him: 'Forgive all our sins and receive us graciously, that we may offer the fruit of our lips.'"

God tells them exactly what to say. He isn't leaving it to chance. He knows they've forgotten how to pray honestly, so he gives them the script. And the words he puts in their mouths are a complete reversal of everything they've been doing. Instead of trusting Assyria, they will say, "Assyria cannot save us." Instead of trusting military power, they will say, "We will not mount warhorses." Instead of trusting idols, they will say, "We will never again say 'our gods' to what our own hands have made."

Then God responds. And his response sounds like spring arriving after the longest winter you've ever endured.

"I will heal their waywardness and love them freely, for my anger has turned away from them. I will be like the dew to Israel; he will blossom like a lily. Like a cedar of Lebanon, he will send down his roots; his young shoots will grow. His splendor will be like an olive tree, his fragrance like a cedar of Lebanon. People will dwell again in his shade; they will flourish like the grain, they will blossom like the vine."

After fourteen chapters of drought and devastation, the garden comes back to life. Lilies bloom. Cedars stretch toward the sky. Olive trees spread their branches. Grain and vines flourish. Every image of barrenness and death that has haunted this book is replaced by an image of growth and abundance.

This is what God wanted all along. Not the punishment. Not the exile. Not the courtroom and the charges. He wanted this: a people who had come home, who had finally stopped running, who could receive his love and flourish in it. The lost child is home again, and everything is growing.

The very last verse of Hosea steps outside the story and speaks directly to the reader: "Who is wise? Let them realize these things. Who is discerning? Let them understand. The ways of the Lord are right; the righteous walk in them, but the rebellious stumble in them."

It's an invitation. Everything you've just read—every warning, every promise, every heartbreaking image of a God who loves people who don't love him back—it's all been leading to this question: What will you do with it? The wise person hears and walks in God's ways. The rebellious person hears and stumbles. Same God. Same message. Different responses.

The choice is yours.

WHAT THIS MEANS FOR US

First, God's love is parental, not transactional. The image of God teaching Israel to walk, lifting them to his cheek, bending down to feed them, these aren't the actions of a business partner. They're the actions of a parent. God doesn't love you because of what you can do for him. He loves you the way a mother or father loves a child who can't do anything yet except be loved. If you've ever wondered whether God's affection for you depends on your performance, chapter 11 is your answer. It doesn't.

Second, God's mercy comes from who he is, not from who we are. "I am God, and not a man." That's the reason he gives for not destroying Israel. His mercy isn't a response to their goodness. It's an expression of his nature. When you feel like you've messed up too badly for God to forgive you, remember that his forgiveness doesn't depend on the size of your failure. It depends on the size of his character. And his character has no limits.

Third, it's never too late to come home. Chapter 14 proves this. After everything Israel did, after every betrayal, every idol, every broken promise, God still says, "Return." He even tells them what words to use. He makes coming home as easy as possible. If you've drifted from God, the path back is not complicated. It starts with honesty: "Forgive all our sins." And it ends with trust: "Receive us graciously." God is not standing at the door with his arms crossed. He's standing at the door with his arms open.

Fourth, the story of Hosea points straight to Jesus. A God who pays the price to buy back people who have betrayed him. A father who keeps loving a child who keeps running away. A promise that death itself will be defeated. A love that is given freely, not earned. Every one of these themes reaches its fullest expression in the life, death, and resurrection of Jesus. Hosea didn't know the name, but he was describing the gospel.

TALKING POINTS

1. **God describes himself as a parent who taught Israel to walk and lifted them to his cheek.** How does picturing God as a loving parent change the way you think about him? Is it easier or harder for you to relate to God as a father than as a king? Why?

2. **God says, "I am God, and not a man," as his reason for showing mercy instead of destruction.** What does this tell you about the difference between human love and divine love? Have you ever experienced a love that went beyond what you thought you deserved?

3. **In chapter 13, Hosea describes God as a lion, a leopard, and a bear. In chapter 14, he describes God as dew, a lily, and a cedar tree.** How can the same God be both? What do these very different images teach us about his character?

4. **God gives Israel the exact words to pray when they come back to him.** Why do you think he does that? Have you ever been in a situation where you wanted to apologize but didn't know what to say? How does it help to know that God doesn't expect you to figure it out on your own?

5. **The last verse of Hosea asks, "Who is wise?" and challenges the reader to respond to everything they've just heard.** Now that you've read through the whole book of Hosea, what stands out to you most? What's one thing about God's character in this book that you don't want to forget?

The book of Hosea began with a wedding and ended with a homecoming. Between those two images lay an entire nation's worth of sin, heartbreak, and stubborn grace. God loved a people who didn't love him back. He disciplined them, pursued them, fought for them, and never once let them go. And when they finally came home, he healed their waywardness and loved them freely.

That's the message Hosea carried for forty years. And it's still true today.

But Hosea isn't the only voice crying out in this era. Another prophet is about to step forward with a different kind of warning. The day of the Lord is coming, and it's closer than anyone thinks.

Turn the page.

4

THE DAY EVERYTHING WENT DARK

Near the end of Disney's *Bambi*, fire comes to the forest. There's no warning, no buildup. One moment the woods are quiet. The next, flames are racing through the trees, consuming everything in their path. The animals run, terrified, crashing through underbrush and leaping over streams. Smoke fills the sky. The forest that has been home to every creature in the story, the place where Bambi was born, where he learned to walk, where the seasons turned in their gentle rhythm, is burning to the ground.

If the movie ended there, it would be unbearable. But it doesn't. After the fire, after the devastation, after the long silence of winter, something happens. Spring arrives. Green shoots push up through the blackened soil. Flowers bloom where the flames had raged. New fawns are born. The forest isn't just repaired. It's renewed. Life comes back stronger than the fire that tried to destroy it.

The book of Joel tells that same story, but on a much larger scale and with far higher stakes. A devastating natural disaster strikes the land of Judah and strips it bare. The prophet interprets the disaster as a warning from God. He calls the people to repentance. They respond. And what God promises on the other side of the devastation isn't just recovery. It's a future so extraordinary that it includes the outpouring of his Spirit on all people and the final defeat of evil itself.

Joel is only three chapters long, but it packs more theological weight per page than almost any book in the Bible. And it all starts with bugs.

A PLAGUE LIKE NO OTHER

Joel opens with a question aimed at the oldest people in the nation: "Has anything like this ever happened in your days, or in the days of your ancestors?" The answer was no. What had just hit the land of Judah was unprecedented. A locust swarm of staggering proportions had swept through the country and devoured everything.

If you've never seen a locust swarm, it's hard to imagine the scale. Locusts are a species of grasshopper that migrates in massive clouds. A single swarm can cover hundreds of square miles and contain billions of insects. Each locust eats its own body weight in food every day. They strip fields bare in hours. They eat the grain, the grapes, the figs, the olives. They eat the leaves off the trees, then they eat the bark. When they're done, what was a lush, green landscape looks like a wasteland. Nothing is left.

Joel describes the destruction in wave after wave. What one swarm left, the next one ate. What that one left, another finished off. The grapevines were gone, so there was no wine. The fig trees were stripped white, their bark peeled off and thrown to the ground. The grain was destroyed, so there was no bread. The olive harvest failed, so there was no oil. Even the livestock were suffering because the pastures had been chewed down to bare dirt.

But Joel wasn't just describing an agricultural disaster. He was reading the signs. The locust plague had cut off the daily offerings at the temple, the sacrifices of grain and wine that were supposed to be presented to God every morning and evening. When those offerings stopped, the connection between God and his people was interrupted. The priests had nothing to bring to the altar. The whole system of worship that held the nation's relationship with God together had ground to a halt.

For Joel, this wasn't a coincidence. This was a message.

THE DAY OF THE LORD

Joel saw in the locust plague something far more significant than a natural disaster. He saw a preview of what the Bible calls "the day of the Lord."

That phrase shows up over and over in the prophets. It refers to a time when God steps into history to judge evil and set things right. Some of Joel's listeners probably thought the day of the Lord would be great news for them, a day when God would crush Israel's enemies and reward his people. The prophet Amos had already corrected that idea a generation or two earlier: "Why do you long for the day of the Lord? That day will be darkness, not light."

Joel agreed. And he made the connection explicit. He told the people to sound the alarm trumpet on the temple mount, because the day of the Lord was not far off. It was near. And its advance guard had already arrived in the form of billions of locusts.

In chapter 2, Joel describes the locust swarm a second time, but now the language shifts into something more intense. The locusts become an army. They advance like soldiers in formation. They scale walls. They enter houses through windows. The ground shakes before them. The sky goes dark as their bodies blot out the sun and moon. The description blurs the line between the literal plague and something cosmic, something apocalyptic. Joel is using the real disaster his people had just lived through as a window into a larger reality: the terrifying power of God when he moves in judgment.

And at the end of this description, Joel asks the question that hangs over the entire book: "The day of the Lord is great; it is dreadful. Who can endure it?"

The answer, on their own, is nobody. But God doesn't leave them there.

REND YOUR HEART

Immediately after the most terrifying passage in the book, God's voice breaks through with an invitation: "Even now, return to me with all your heart, with fasting and weeping and mourning."

Even now. Even after everything. Even in the middle of the devastation. It's not too late.

But God doesn't want a performance. He wants something real. "Rend your heart and not your garments," he says. In Israel's culture, people tore their clothes as a sign of grief and repentance. It was visible and dramatic. God is saying: I don't want torn clothes. I want a torn heart. I want genuine sorrow, not a public display. I want you to actually change, not just look like you're changing.

Then comes one of the most important descriptions of God's character in the entire Old Testament: "Return to the Lord your God, for he is gracious and compassionate, slow to anger and abounding in love, and he relents from sending calamity." This isn't new information. It goes all the way back to what God revealed about himself to Moses on Mount Sinai after the golden calf disaster. But Joel repeats it here because the people need to hear it again. The God who sends judgment is the same God whose nature is mercy. His default setting is compassion. Judgment is what happens when people push him away. But his arms are always open for those who come back.

Joel then calls for a national assembly. Everyone is to gather at the temple. The elderly. The children. Even nursing infants. Even newlyweds who would normally be excused from public duties. Nobody gets a pass. The crisis is too severe for anyone to sit this one out. The priests are to stand between the temple entrance and the altar, weeping and praying: "Spare your people, Lord. Do not make your inheritance an object of scorn, a byword among the nations. Why should they say among the peoples, 'Where is their God?'"

That last question is the sharpest one in the prayer. If God doesn't act, his own reputation is on the line. The surrounding nations will conclude that Israel's God is powerless. And that's something God will not allow.

THE YEARS THE LOCUSTS HAVE EATEN

Between the end of the prayer and the beginning of God's response, something happened. The text doesn't describe it, but we can piece it together. The people listened to Joel. They gathered. They fasted. They repented. And God responded.

"Then the Lord was jealous for his land and took pity on his people."

That single sentence is the turning point of the entire book. Everything before it is devastation and warning. Everything after it is restoration and promise.

God's response is specific and generous. He promises to send grain, new wine, and olive oil, the exact things the locusts had destroyed. He promises to drive the locust army into the desert and the sea, where they will rot. He promises that the pastures will turn green again, the trees will bear fruit, and the autumn and spring rains will fall on schedule.

Then comes the line that people have clung to for centuries: "I will repay you for the years the locusts have eaten."

Those words reach far beyond agriculture. They speak to anyone who has watched something precious get destroyed, whether by their own mistakes, by someone else's cruelty, or by circumstances beyond their control. God is not just a God who forgives. He is a God who restores. He gives back what was lost. Not always in the same form, not always on our timeline, but he makes the broken years count for something.

The restoration section ends with a ringing declaration: "You will know that I am in the midst of Israel, that I am the Lord your God, and that there is no other." That's the whole point. The disaster, the repentance, the restoration, all of it was designed to bring the people back to one foundational truth: God is real, he is present, and there is no one else like him.

THE SPIRIT POURED OUT

But God isn't finished. He has something planned that goes far beyond fixing locust damage.

"And afterward, I will pour out my Spirit on all people. Your sons and daughters will prophesy, your old men will dream dreams, your young men will see visions. Even on my servants, both men and women, I will pour out my Spirit in those days."

This is one of the most revolutionary promises in the Old Testament. Up to this point, God's Spirit had been given to specific individuals for specific tasks: kings, prophets, priests, warriors. It was selective and temporary. Now God is promising to pour out his Spirit on everyone. Sons and daughters. Old and young. Masters and servants. No distinction by gender, age, or social class. Everyone who belongs to God will have direct access to his presence and his power.

Joel's original audience might have understood this as a promise limited to Israel. But when the day of Pentecost came, centuries later, the apostle Peter stood up in Jerusalem and quoted this exact passage to explain what was happening. The Holy Spirit was falling on people from every nation, and Peter said, "This is what was spoken by the prophet Joel." The promise turned out to be even bigger than anyone had imagined. God's Spirit wasn't just for Israel. It was for the whole world.

Joel also describes cosmic signs that will accompany these events: the sun turning to darkness, the moon to blood, wonders in the heavens and on the earth. These images of upheaval signal that God is doing something so massive it shakes the very foundations of creation.

And then the promise that holds it all together: "Everyone who calls on the name of the Lord will be saved." Paul quoted this line in his letter to the Romans to make the case that salvation is available to anyone, Jew or Gentile, who trusts and obeys Jesus. What Joel spoke as a promise to a locust-ravaged nation became one of the most quoted verses in the entire New Testament.

THE VALLEY OF DECISION

The final chapter of Joel shifts from Israel to the nations. God announces that he will gather all the nations to a place called the Valley of Jehoshaphat, a name that means "the Lord judges." There he will hold them accountable for how they treated his people. They scattered Israel among the nations. They divided up the land. They sold children into slavery for the price of an evening's pleasure. God has seen it all, and he will repay.

Joel calls the nations to assemble for battle, but the irony is devastating. "Beat your plowshares into swords and your pruning hooks into spears," he says, deliberately reversing the famous promise from Isaiah and Micah about turning weapons into farming tools. The age of peace hasn't arrived yet. First comes judgment. And the nations who have spent centuries oppressing God's people are about to discover what it means to face God himself in the courtroom.

"Multitudes, multitudes in the valley of decision! For the day of the Lord is near in the valley of decision." The word "decision" here means verdict. The nations have made their choices. Now God makes his.

GOD DWELLS IN ZION

The book ends not with judgment but with a vision of what lies beyond it. Joel describes a restored land where the mountains drip with wine, the hills flow with milk, and a fountain pours out from the house of the Lord to water even the driest valleys. Egypt and Edom, ancient enemies of God's people, will become wastelands. But Judah will be inhabited forever.

The very last line of the book delivers the message that everything else has been building toward: "The Lord dwells in Zion!"

That's it. That's the whole point. The locusts came and the offerings stopped and it looked like God had abandoned his people. But he hadn't. He was using the disaster to bring them back to himself. And when they came back, he didn't just restore what was lost. He promised something new: his Spirit on all flesh, his presence among his people forever, and a future where every wrong would be made right.

The God who seemed absent was there the whole time. And he's not going anywhere.

WHAT THIS MEANS FOR US

First, God can use disaster to get our attention. The locust plague wasn't random bad luck. Joel saw it as God's megaphone, amplifying a message the people had been ignoring. When life falls apart, our first instinct is usually to ask, "Why is this happening?" Joel suggests a better question: "What is God trying to say?" Not every hardship is divine punishment, but every hardship is an opportunity to turn back to God and listen.

Second, God wants real repentance, not religious performance. Torn clothes are easy. A torn heart is hard. It's possible to go through all the motions of faith, to show up, to say the right words, to look the part, and still have a heart that hasn't actually changed. God sees the difference. He always has.

Third, no season of loss is beyond God's ability to restore. "I will repay you for the years the locusts have eaten" is a promise that applies to more than crops. It applies to wasted years, broken relationships, lost opportunities, and seasons of spiritual drought. God doesn't just forgive the past. He redeems it. He finds a way to make even the lost years count.

Fourth, the Spirit of God is for everyone. Joel's promise shattered every barrier: gender, age, social class. When the Spirit came at Pentecost, it confirmed that God's presence isn't reserved for a spiritual elite. It's for every person who calls on his name. That includes you.

TALKING POINTS

1. **Joel saw the locust plague as more than a natural disaster. He saw it as a message from God.** How do you decide whether a difficult event in your life is just something that happened or something God is using to get your attention? Is there a difference?

2. **God told the people to "rend your heart and not your garments."** What does it look like to go through the outward motions of faith without really meaning it? How can you tell the difference between genuine repentance and just performing for an audience?

3. **"I will repay you for the years the locusts have eaten."** What does this promise mean to you personally? Is there a season of loss in your life that you'd like to see God restore?

4. **Joel promised that God would pour out his Spirit on "all people," breaking barriers of gender, age, and social status.** Why do you think this was such a radical promise? What does it mean for the way we think about who gets to participate in God's work today?

5. **The book of Joel ends with the declaration "The Lord dwells in Zion."** After everything the people went through, why is God's presence the most important part of the restoration? What would change in your life if you really believed that God is present with you right now?

Joel's locust plague is over. God's Spirit has been promised. The day of the Lord has been revealed in all its terror and all its hope. But the prophetic voices of this era are far from finished. Another prophet is about to step forward, and this one isn't a priest or a professional. He's a shepherd and a farmer, and he has a message about justice that will make the powerful very uncomfortable.

Turn the page.

5

THE TRAP

Picture this. You're sitting in class, and the teacher starts telling the story of a student who cheated on a test. She doesn't name names. She just describes what the student did, how they copied answers, how they lied about it, how they got caught. The whole class is shaking their heads. "That's so wrong," someone whispers. "I can't believe anyone would do that." Everybody's nodding. Everybody agrees. Cheating is terrible. The person who did it should be ashamed.

Then the teacher pauses, looks around the room, and says: "The student I'm describing is in this class."

Suddenly the mood changes. People stop nodding. They start looking at each other. Wait. Is she talking about me? The comfortable distance between "that terrible person" and "us" has just collapsed.

That's exactly what the prophet Amos did. He stood up in the northern kingdom of Israel, started preaching about the sins of Israel's enemies, and let the crowd cheer along as nation after nation was condemned. Then he turned the spotlight on Israel itself, and the audience realized they'd walked straight into a trap.

It's one of the most brilliant pieces of prophetic preaching in the entire Bible. And it comes from a man nobody expected to hear from.

A FARMER WITH A MESSAGE

Amos was not a priest. He was not a professional prophet. He was not trained at any school of ministry. He was a farmer from Tekoa, a small town in the southern kingdom of Judah, about ten miles south of Jerusalem, perched on the edge of a vast and barren wilderness that dropped four thousand feet down to the Dead Sea. It was rugged country, and the people who lived there were rugged too.

Amos raised livestock. The word used to describe him in the original text isn't the ordinary word for a shepherd watching a few sheep. It's a word that suggests someone in the sheep and cattle business on a larger scale. He also tended sycamore-fig trees, a crop that grew in the lowlands and required hands-on labor to cultivate. He was a working man, and probably a successful one.

But around 760 BC, God interrupted his life with a call Amos never asked for. "Go," God said, "and prophesy to my people Israel." Not Judah, his home country. Israel. The northern kingdom. A foreign nation with its own king, its own worship centers, and its own religious establishment, none of which had any interest in hearing bad news from a southern farmer.

Amos went anyway. And what he had to say would make him one of the most hated men in the country.

A NATION THAT LOOKED UNSTOPPABLE

To understand why Amos' message hit so hard, you need to understand how good things looked in Israel at the time. King Jeroboam II had been on the throne for decades. The economy was booming. The borders were expanding. Israel had recovered territory it had lost to its enemies, and the wealth was pouring in. The rich were building stone mansions and decorating them with ivory. The markets were busy. The worship centers were packed.

From the outside, Israel looked like a nation blessed by God.

But Amos saw what was underneath. The wealth was concentrated in the hands of a few powerful families while the poor were being crushed. Merchants cheated their customers. Judges took bribes. Creditors sold people into slavery over tiny debts. The courts, which were supposed to protect the vulnerable, had become tools of the powerful. And the religion that should have challenged all of this was instead providing cover for it. People showed up at the temples, offered their sacrifices, celebrated their festivals, and went right back to exploiting their neighbors.

God had seen enough. And Amos was the messenger he sent.

THE SERMON THAT SET THE TRAP

When Amos opened his mouth to preach, his first words were not about Israel. They were about Israel's enemies. And that was deliberate.

"The Lord roars from Zion," Amos began, "and thunders from Jerusalem." Already the audience might have bristled. Zion and Jerusalem were in Judah, the southern kingdom. To say God roared from there, and not from Israel's worship centers at Bethel or Samaria, was a jab at their national pride. But they kept listening, because what came next sounded like exactly what they wanted to hear.

"For three sins of Damascus, even for four, I will not relent." Damascus. Israel's old enemy to the northeast. The Arameans had invaded Israel's territory, brutalized its people, and dragged threshing sledges over their victims in Gilead. God would send fire on Damascus. The crowd roared with approval.

Then the Philistines. They had raided Israelite towns, kidnapped entire communities, and sold them as slaves. God would send fire on their cities too. Gaza, Ashdod, Ashkelon, Ekron. They would all pay.

Then Tyre, the wealthy Phoenician port city to the northwest. They had participated in the slave trade and broken a treaty of friendship. Fire on Tyre.

The audience was loving this. Every nation Amos named was one they had reason to hate. One by one, their enemies were being called to account by the God of Israel. This prophet from Judah was saying exactly what they wanted to hear.

CLOSER AND CLOSER

But Amos wasn't finished. And the nations he named next were getting closer to home.

Edom. Israel's ancient rival to the south, descended from Esau, Jacob's own brother. Edom had pursued Israel with a sword, showing no mercy, stifling all compassion. The family connection made the cruelty even worse. God would send fire on Edom's strongholds.

Ammon. East of the Jordan River. They had ripped open pregnant women in Gilead to expand their territory, an act of violence so extreme it still sickened everyone who heard it. Fire on Ammon's capital, Rabbah.

Moab. South of Ammon. They had desecrated the bones of an Edomite king, burning them to lime as a final act of disrespect. Even the dead were not safe from their contempt. Fire on Moab.

And then Judah. Amos' own country. "For three sins of Judah, even for four, I will not relent. They have rejected the law of the Lord and have not kept his decrees." The crowd might have cheered even louder at this one. Even the prophet's homeland was condemned.

By now the pattern was unmistakable. Every nation surrounding Israel was under judgment. God was sweeping through the region like a fire, and every enemy Israel had ever known was being consumed. The Israelites in the crowd probably thought they were watching God prepare to bless them. They were the ones left standing while everyone else burned.

They were wrong.

THE TRAP SPRINGS SHUT

"For three sins of Israel, even for four, I will not relent."

You can almost feel the air leave the room. Israel? Us? After seven nations had been condemned, after the crowd had cheered every indictment, the eighth and final charge lands on them. And it is the longest and most detailed accusation of all.

"They sell the innocent for silver, and the needy for a pair of sandals." People were being sold into debt slavery over amounts so small they were barely worth mentioning. A pair of sandals. That's what a human life was worth in Israel's courts.

"They trample on the heads of the poor as on the dust of the ground and deny justice to the oppressed." The powerful didn't just neglect the poor. They ground them into the dirt. The legal system that was supposed to protect the vulnerable had been twisted into a weapon against them.

"Father and son use the same girl." Whether this describes incest, exploitation of a servant, or involvement in pagan worship practices, the result is the same: God's name was being profaned by the behavior of people who called themselves his.

"They lie down beside every altar on garments taken in pledge." The law required that if you took a poor person's coat as collateral for a loan, you had to give it back before nightfall so they could sleep in it. Instead, the wealthy were keeping those garments and using them as cushions while they lounged at their altars, sipping wine purchased with money squeezed from the poor through unjust fines.

The contrast between Israel's crimes and those of the surrounding nations is striking. The other nations were judged for war atrocities: torture, slave-trading, desecrating the dead. Israel was judged for something that might seem less dramatic but was, in God's eyes, just as wicked: the systematic oppression of the poor and the corruption of justice. And Israel's crimes were worse in one crucial way. The other nations didn't have a covenant with God. Israel did. They knew better. They had the law. They had the prophets. They had the history of God's faithfulness stretching back to the exodus. And they still chose injustice.

NO ESCAPE

God reminds Israel of everything he did for them. He destroyed the Amorites who stood in their way, towering people whose strength was legendary. He brought them out of Egypt. He led them through the wilderness for forty years. He raised up prophets to speak his word and Nazirites to model devotion. And what did Israel do? They made the Nazirites drink wine, breaking their vows. They told the prophets, "Stop prophesying." They silenced the very voices God had sent to save them.

So now the judgment falls. And Amos describes it in terms his audience would have understood immediately, because Israel took enormous pride in its military. He lists seven types of soldiers: the swift, the strong, the warrior, the archer, the fleet-footed, the horseman, the brave. Every category of fighting man. And not one of them will escape. The swift will not be fast enough. The strong will lose their strength. The warrior will not save his own life. The archer will not stand his ground. The horseman will not ride away. Even the bravest soldier will throw down his weapons and run naked into the night.

The message is total. There will be no escape. The nation that thought God's judgment was reserved for its enemies has just discovered that the same standard applies to them. The trap that Amos set with his opening words has snapped shut, and Israel is caught.

WHAT THIS MEANS FOR US

First, nobody gets a free pass. Israel assumed that being God's chosen people made them exempt from judgment. Amos shattered that illusion. Being close to God doesn't give you permission to ignore his standards. If anything, it raises the bar. "You only have I chosen of all the families of the earth," God will say in the next chapter. "Therefore I will punish you for all your sins." Privilege doesn't reduce accountability. It increases it.

Second, how we treat the vulnerable reveals who we really are. Israel's sins weren't exotic. They were economic. They were legal. They were the kinds of injustice that happen when the powerful stop caring about the powerless. Selling people for the price of sandals, rigging the courts, keeping a poor person's only coat. These are the sins God took most seriously. And they're the sins that are easiest to overlook because they don't look dramatic from the outside.

Third, pointing fingers is easy. Seeing your own guilt is hard. The crowd cheered when Amos condemned their enemies. They only went silent when he condemned them. We do the same thing. It's always easier to see the sin in someone else's life than in our own. Amos' sermon is a reminder that the finger eventually points back at us.

Fourth, God's patience has a limit. The phrase "for three sins, even for four" isn't just a poetic formula. It communicates that God has been counting. He has seen the injustice pile up, one offense after another, and there comes a point where he says, "Enough." That doesn't mean God is eager to punish. It means he takes evil seriously and will not let it go on forever.

TALKING POINTS

1. **Amos set a rhetorical trap by condemning Israel's enemies first.** Why do you think the crowd was so eager to hear

judgment on other nations? Why is it satisfying to hear that someone else is in trouble, and what does that say about us?

2. **The surrounding nations were judged for war crimes and slave-trading. Israel was judged for economic injustice and corruption in the courts.** Why do you think God treated these as equally serious? What does this tell you about how God views the way we treat people in everyday life?

3. **Amos was a farmer, not a professional prophet. God called him out of his normal life to deliver a message nobody wanted to hear.** What does this say about who God can use? Have you ever felt like you weren't qualified for something God was asking you to do?

4. **God reminded Israel of everything he had done for them before announcing judgment.** Why do you think he did that? How does remembering what God has done for you change the way you respond when you realize you've been wrong?

5. **The seven types of soldiers who couldn't escape represent total judgment. No strength, speed, or bravery could save them.** Why is this an important message for people who think they can handle the consequences of sin on their own? What's the only real escape Amos points toward?

The trap has sprung. Israel now knows that the same God who judges the nations is judging them. But Amos isn't finished. In the chapters ahead, he will lay out exactly what went wrong, from the courtrooms to the marketplaces to the worship centers, and he will issue one of the most powerful calls for justice ever recorded.

Turn the page.

6

JUSTICE ROLLS DOWN

Charles Dickens opened *A Tale of Two Cities* with one of the most famous sentences in literature: "It was the best of times, it was the worst of times." He was describing France on the eve of its revolution, a nation where the wealthy threw lavish parties while the poor starved in the streets. The aristocrats lived in gilded mansions. They wore silk and drank expensive wine and spent more on a single dinner than most families saw in a year. And they assumed it would last forever.

It didn't. The revolution came because the people at the bottom had been crushed for too long by the people at the top, and the whole system collapsed under the weight of its own injustice.

Amos could have written that opening line about Israel. In the middle of the eighth century BC, Israel was experiencing the best of times and the worst of times at the same moment. The rich were getting richer. The poor were getting poorer. The powerful were building summer homes and decorating them with ivory while families a few streets over were being sold into slavery over unpaid debts. The courts were corrupt. The worship centers were packed with people who loved religion but hated justice. And nobody at the top seemed to notice, or care, that the whole thing was about to come crashing down.

Amos noticed. And in chapters 3–6, he lays out the full case against Israel with a precision and a fury that still burns off the page.

CHOSEN, THEREFORE JUDGED

The first thing Amos establishes is that Israel's special relationship with God doesn't protect them from judgment. It guarantees it.

"You only have I chosen of all the families of the earth," God says. "Therefore I will punish you for all your sins."

That word "therefore" lands like a hammer. The people of Israel believed that being chosen by God meant being shielded by God. They assumed that the covenant was a security blanket. No matter what they did, God would never let anything bad happen to his people.

Amos flips that logic on its head. Being chosen doesn't mean being excused. It means being held to a higher standard. God had invested more in Israel than in any other nation. He had rescued them from Egypt, led them through the wilderness, given them the land, sent them prophets. And they had responded by building an entire society on the backs of the poor. The greater the privilege, the greater the accountability.

WHEN THE LION ROARS

Amos drives his point home with a rapid-fire series of questions that all make the same point: every effect has a cause.

Do two people walk together unless they've agreed to meet? Does a lion roar in the forest when it has no prey? Does a bird fall into a trap where no snare has been set? Does a trumpet sound in a city without the people trembling?

The questions build from everyday life to something ominous. And then Amos delivers the punch line: "When a lion roars, who will not fear? The Sovereign Lord has spoken. Who can but prophesy?" Amos didn't choose to be a prophet. He didn't volunteer for this assignment. The lion roared, and he had no choice but to speak. What's coming is as inevitable as the cause behind every effect in his list.

Then God does something astonishing. He invites the people of Ashdod and Egypt, two of Israel's pagan neighbors, to come and sit on the mountains around Samaria and watch what's happening inside the capital. Even these nations, famous for their own injustice, will be shocked by what they see. The violence and oppression inside Israel's walls are so extreme that outsiders who don't even know God's law can recognize that something is deeply wrong.

When your enemies are appalled by your behavior, you have a serious problem.

IVORY AND ASHES

The picture Amos paints of Samaria's wealthy class is vivid. They lounge on beds inlaid with ivory. They eat choice lamb and fattened calves. They have winter homes and summer homes. Their mansions are decorated with imported luxuries. And all of it has been built on stolen wealth, extracted from the poor through rigged courts and predatory lending.

God says he will tear it all down. The great houses will be demolished. The altars at Bethel, Israel's most important worship center, will have their horns cut off, which means the place of mercy and sanctuary will be destroyed. When judgment comes, there will be nowhere to run.

In one of his most cutting images, Amos compares the coming destruction to a shepherd trying to rescue a sheep from a lion. All the shepherd manages to pull from the lion's mouth are two leg bones and a piece of an ear. That's all that will be left of Israel. Not a kingdom. Not a city. Just scraps.

COWS AND EMPTY ALTARS

Chapter 4 opens with a line that must have made the wealthy women of Samaria furious. Amos calls them "cows of Bashan," comparing them to the pampered, well-fed cattle that grazed on the lush pastures east of the Jordan. These women were living in luxury, demanding that their husbands bring them more wine, while the poor outside their doors were being crushed. God swears by his own holiness that they will be dragged away through holes in the city walls when the enemy comes.

Then Amos turns to the worship centers with blistering sarcasm. "Go to Bethel and sin!" he says. "Go to Gilgal and sin some more! Bring your sacrifices every morning, your tithes every three days. Brag about your freewill offerings. Boast about them! This is what you love to do, Israel."

The Israelites loved their religion. They loved the festivals, the music, the rituals. What they didn't love was the God behind it all, or the justice he demanded. Their worship was a performance, an exercise in self-congratulation. They showed up, offered their sacrifices, and went home feeling righteous, all without changing a single thing about the way they treated people.

FIVE WARNINGS, ONE RESPONSE

God then lists five disasters he had sent to wake Israel up. Empty stomachs. Drought that hit some cities while sparing others. Crops destroyed by blight, mildew, and locusts. Plague and war. A brush with total destruction, like Sodom and Gomorrah.

After each one, the same refrain: "Yet you have not returned to me."

Five times God said it. Five warnings. Five chances to turn around. And five times Israel shrugged it off and kept going. They didn't connect the dots between their suffering and their sin. They didn't see God's hand behind the hardship. Or maybe they saw it and simply didn't care.

The section closes with words that must have sent a chill through anyone who was paying attention: "Therefore this is what I will do to you, Israel. Prepare to meet your God."

SEEK ME AND LIVE

Chapter 5 opens with a funeral. Not a literal one. Amos sings a lament, a death song, for a nation that is still alive. "Fallen is Virgin Israel, never to rise again, deserted in her own land, with no one to lift her up." He's mourning a country that hasn't died yet, because in his prophetic vision, its destruction is already certain.

But even here, in the darkest moment of the book, God leaves a door open. "Seek me and live," he says. Don't seek Bethel. Don't seek Gilgal. Don't seek Beersheba. Those places are finished. Seek the Lord himself. "Seek good, not evil, that you may live. Hate evil, love good; maintain justice in the courts. Perhaps the Lord God Almighty will have mercy on the remnant of Joseph."

That word "perhaps" is honest. God doesn't promise that repentance will undo every consequence. But he holds open the possibility that a faithful few, a remnant, might survive what's coming.

At the center of this section sits the verse that has echoed through the centuries more loudly than any other in the book: "But let justice roll on like a river, righteousness like a never-failing stream."

In a region where most riverbeds were dry wadis that only ran with water after a rain, the image of a never-failing stream was extraordinary. God wasn't asking for an occasional act of fairness when it was convenient. He was demanding a constant, unstoppable flow of justice through every corner of society, as reliable as a river that never runs dry. Martin Luther King Jr. quoted this verse in his "I Have a Dream" speech, because the demand it makes is as urgent now as it was in the eighth century BC.

DARKNESS, NOT LIGHT

Amos then takes aim at the popular belief that the "day of the Lord" would be a day of celebration, a day when God would defeat all of Israel's enemies and exalt his people. The crowd at the worship centers couldn't wait for that day.

Amos tells them they're fools to want it. "Why do you long for the day of the Lord? That day will be darkness, not light."

Then he paints a picture of inescapable doom: a man runs from a lion and meets a bear. He reaches his house, leans against the wall to catch his breath, and a snake bites him. There is no safe place. The day of the Lord will not be what they expect.

And God makes his rejection of Israel's worship explicit: "I hate, I despise your religious festivals. Your assemblies are a stench to me. Even though you bring me offerings, I will not accept them. Away with the noise of your songs! I will not listen to the music of your harps."

These are among the most severe words in the entire Bible. God is rejecting worship that has been divorced from justice. The festivals are real. The offerings are genuine. The music is skilled. And God hates all of it, because the people who bring these gifts are the same people who trample the poor and pervert the courts. Worship without justice is not worship. It's a cover story.

WOE TO THE COMFORTABLE

Chapter 6 targets the elite directly. "Woe to you who are complacent in Zion, and to you who feel secure on Mount Samaria." The leaders of both kingdoms are named. They lounge on ivory beds. They eat the best meat. They improvise on musical instruments like David, as if their artistic talent excuses their moral failure. They drink wine by the bowlful and anoint themselves with the finest lotions.

And then the line that makes the whole scene unbearable: "But you do not grieve over the ruin of Joseph." They do not grieve. The nation is falling apart around them. The poor are being crushed. The courts are broken. The prophets have been silenced. And the people with the power to do something about it are too busy enjoying themselves to notice.

Therefore, Amos says, they will be the first to go into exile. The party is over. The feasting will end. And the people who refused to feel the suffering of others will be the ones who feel the judgment most.

Amos closes with a pair of sarcastic questions: "Do horses run on rocky crags? Does anyone plow the sea with oxen?" The answer is obviously no. Those things are absurd. And yet, Amos says, you have done something equally absurd: "You have turned justice into poison and the fruit of righteousness into bitterness." You have taken the very things that were supposed to sustain your society and turned them into weapons. That is not just wrong. It is insane.

WHAT THIS MEANS FOR US

First, privilege demands responsibility. Israel thought that being God's chosen people meant being God's protected people. Amos corrected them. Being close to God means being held to God's standard. This applies to anyone who has been given much: much is expected in return.

Second, worship without justice is meaningless. God doesn't want our songs if we're hurting people on the way to church. He doesn't want our offerings if we're ignoring the needs around us. Real worship flows into real justice. If it doesn't, it's not real worship.

Third, God notices what the powerful ignore. The wealthy in Samaria didn't grieve over the ruin of the poor. God did. He saw every rigged court case, every stolen coat, every family sold into slavery. The fact that the powerful didn't notice doesn't mean nobody noticed. God always sees.

Fourth, justice isn't optional. It's not a nice addition to the spiritual life. It's the river that's supposed to run through everything. "Let justice roll on like a river, righteousness like a never-failing stream." Not a trickle. Not when it's convenient. A river. Always flowing, always present, always shaping the landscape around it.

TALKING POINTS

1. **God told Israel, "You only have I chosen, therefore I will punish you."** Why does being close to God increase your responsibility rather than decrease it? Can you think of examples in your own life where having more privilege meant being held to a higher standard?

2. **The wealthy women of Samaria were called "cows of Bashan" because they lived in luxury while the poor suffered.** What does it look like today when people enjoy comfort without considering those who are struggling? How can you avoid that kind of blindness?

3. **Five times God said, "Yet you have not returned to me."** What does it take to get your attention when you've drifted away from God? Have you ever gone through a hard time and only later realized God was trying to get your attention?

4. **"Let justice roll on like a river, righteousness like a never-failing stream."** What does justice look like in your school, your neighborhood, or your friend group? What's one specific way you could help justice "roll on" this week?

5. **God said he hated Israel's worship because it was disconnected from how they treated people.** How do you think God feels about religious activity that ignores injustice? What's the connection between loving God and loving your neighbor?

The charges have been made. The case is airtight. Israel's injustice has been exposed from the courtroom to the marketplace to the temple itself. But Amos has one more thing to show them: five visions of what's coming next, and a confrontation with the most powerful priest in the land that will force him to choose between silence and obedience.

Turn the page.

7

THE VISIONS AND THE END

Disney's *Pinocchio* is a story about warnings that keep getting worse. The wooden puppet wants to be a real boy, but he keeps wandering into danger despite every signal telling him to stop. First, Jiminy Cricket tries to steer him right, and Pinocchio ignores him. Then Stromboli locks him in a cage, and he barely escapes. Then he ends up on Pleasure Island, where the fun turns to horror as boys are transformed into donkeys, and the audience realizes that every ignored warning led somewhere darker than the last. The stakes escalate with each scene. What started as a small detour from the right path ends in a nightmare.

The final section of Amos works the same way. God gives the prophet five visions, and each one is worse than the one before. In the first two, Amos begs God to hold back, and God relents. By the third, the pleading stops. By the fourth, the end has arrived. And by the fifth, God is standing at the altar of Israel's most sacred worship center, giving the order to tear it down. The warnings have escalated to their final stage, and time has run out.

But like Pinocchio, the story doesn't end in the nightmare. After the darkest vision comes a promise so unexpected it changes the entire meaning of the book. Before we get there, though, we have to walk through the darkness.

THE FIRST TWO VISIONS: MERCY HOLDS

In the first vision, God shows Amos a swarm of locusts devouring the land. The timing is devastating. The king has already taken his share of the first harvest, and now the locusts are destroying the second crop, the one the ordinary people depend on for survival. The poor will starve.

Amos doesn't hesitate. He falls to his knees and prays: "Sovereign Lord, forgive! How can Jacob survive? He is so small!" Amos, the man who had just spent six chapters condemning Israel for its sins, now begs God to have mercy on them. He knows they deserve the judgment. But he also knows they are fragile, and he loves them enough to intercede.

God's response is stunning in its simplicity: "This will not happen." He relents. The vision dissolves. The locusts don't come.

In the second vision, God shows Amos a great fire that devours the deep waters under the earth and begins consuming the land itself. It's even worse than the first vision. Again Amos cries out: "Sovereign Lord, I beg you, stop! How can Jacob survive? He is so small!"

Again God relents: "This will not happen either."

Two visions. Two prayers. Two reprieves. But the pattern is about to break.

THE THIRD VISION: NO MORE MERCY

In the third vision, God is standing beside a wall, holding something in his hand. It was a plumb line, a tool used to check whether a wall is straight. The meaning is clear. God is measuring Israel against his standard, and the nation doesn't measure up. "I will spare them no longer," God says. The holy places will be destroyed. The royal house will fall.

Notice what's missing. Amos doesn't pray. He doesn't intercede. He doesn't beg God to stop. The window of mercy that was open in the first two visions has quietly closed. The prophet who pleaded for his people has gone silent, because he knows the time for pleading is over.

THE FARMER VS. THE PRIEST

What happens next is one of the most dramatic confrontations in the entire Bible.

Amaziah, the chief priest at Bethel, Israel's most important national sanctuary, hears what Amos has been preaching. He sends a message to King Jeroboam II: "Amos is raising a conspiracy against you right in the heart of Israel. The land cannot bear all his words." Then he turns to Amos directly: "Get out, you seer! Go back to the land of Judah. Earn your bread there and do your prophesying there. Don't prophesy anymore at Bethel, because this is the king's sanctuary and the temple of the kingdom."

Amaziah's argument is simple: Bethel belongs to the king. It's a state-sponsored worship center. You're a foreigner. You don't belong here. Leave.

Amos doesn't flinch. "I was neither a prophet nor the son of a prophet," he answers. "I was a shepherd, and I also took care of sycamore-fig trees. But the Lord took me from tending the flock and said to me, 'Go, prophesy to my people Israel.'"

Amos isn't there because he chose to be. He's there because God sent him. He isn't a professional preacher looking for an audience. He's a farmer who left his flocks because the lion roared and he couldn't stay silent. His authority doesn't come from a religious institution or a royal appointment. It comes from God.

Then Amos delivers a personal prophecy to Amaziah that is as specific as it is devastating. Amaziah's wife will be disgraced. His children will be killed. His land will be divided up. And Amaziah himself will die in a foreign country, in exile, far from the land he thought was untouchable. The priest who told the prophet to be quiet would live to see everything the prophet warned about.

THE FOURTH VISION: RIPE FOR JUDGMENT

In the fourth vision, God shows Amos a basket of ripe fruit. In the original language, there's a wordplay here that doesn't translate into English: the word for "ripe fruit" sounds almost identical to the word for "the end." When Amos sees the basket, God says, "The time is ripe for my people Israel. I will spare them no longer."

Ripe fruit normally means harvest time, a season of celebration. But this harvest is judgment. The songs in the temple will turn to wailing. Dead bodies will be everywhere, so many that they'll be thrown out in silence because there are too many to mourn properly.

Then Amos turns to the merchants who have been cheating the poor. He describes them sitting through the Sabbath and the religious festivals, impatient for the holy days to end so they can get back to making money. "When will the New

Moon be over," they mutter, "so we can sell our grain? When will the Sabbath end so we can open our wheat for sale?" And when they do open for business, they cheat. They shrink the measuring baskets. They inflate the prices. They rig the scales. They mix garbage in with the wheat and sell it to the poor, who have no choice but to buy it.

God swears he will never forget a single one of these acts.

What follows is one of the most haunting prophecies in the book. God says he will send "a famine through the land, not a famine of food or a thirst for water, but a famine of hearing the words of the Lord." People will stagger from sea to sea, searching for a word from God, and they will not find it. The prophets they silenced, the messages they refused to hear, the truth they pushed away, it will all be gone. And the silence will be worse than any judgment of fire or locusts, because a world without God's voice is a world without hope.

THE FIFTH VISION: NO ESCAPE

The fifth and final vision is the most terrifying. Amos sees God himself standing beside the altar of the temple, and God gives the command: "Strike the tops of the pillars so that the thresholds shake. Bring them down on the heads of all the people."

The very building where Israel worshiped, the place they believed was the safest spot in the nation, becomes the site of their destruction. The roof collapses on the worshipers. And for anyone who survives the collapse, there is no escape.

Amos describes the futility of running in language that sweeps across the entire universe. If they dig down to the grave, God will reach down and pull them out. If they climb up to the heavens, God will bring them back down. If they hide on the peak of Mount Carmel, God will search them out. If they dive to the bottom of the sea, God will command the serpent to find them. If they are marched away as prisoners, God will send the sword after them there.

"I will fix my eyes upon them for harm and not for good."

There is no corner of creation where a person can hide from the God who made it all. The five visions have reached their terrible conclusion. The first two offered a chance at mercy. The last three offer none.

BUT THEN

And then, after the darkest passage in the entire book, something happens that no one saw coming. "In that day I will restore David's fallen shelter. I will repair its broken walls and restore its ruins, and will build it as it used to be."

After everything. After the locusts and the fire and the plumb line and the ripe fruit and the collapsing temple. After the famine of God's word and the inescapable judgment. After all of it, God promises restoration.

The "fallen shelter" is the dynasty of David, which by Amos' time had been reduced to the small southern kingdom of Judah. But God says he will rebuild it. Not just Israel. Not just Judah. The promise extends to "all the nations that bear my name," a phrase that stretches far beyond ethnic Israel.

Centuries later, when the early church was debating whether non-Jewish believers could be included in God's people, James quoted this exact verse at the council in Jerusalem. He argued that what God had promised through Amos was now being fulfilled: people from every nation were being gathered under God's restored kingdom through Jesus (Acts 15:16–18).

And the final image in the book is breathtaking. After nine chapters of drought and devastation, Amos describes a future of impossible abundance. "The reaper will be overtaken by the plowman and the planter by the one treading grapes. New wine will drip from the mountains and flow from all the hills." The harvests will be so enormous that farmers won't finish gathering one crop before it's time to plant the next. The cities will be rebuilt. The gardens will flourish. And God will plant his people in their own land, "never again to be uprooted."

That's the last word. Not judgment. Not exile. Not silence. Planting. Abundance. Home. The God who roared like a lion in the first verse of the book now kneels like a gardener in the last, pressing seeds into the soil and promising that this time, they will stay.

WHAT THIS MEANS FOR US

First, God's patience is real, but it has a purpose. The first two visions show a God who is willing to relent when someone intercedes. But by the third vision, the time for intercession has passed. God's patience isn't infinite passivity. It's a window of opportunity that we shouldn't take for granted.

Second, faithfulness to God will sometimes cost you. Amos was told to leave, to be quiet, to go home. He refused because his calling came from God, not from a human institution. There will be times when following God puts you in conflict with people in authority. What matters is whose voice you're obeying.

Third, a world without God's word is the worst possible famine. We can survive without food longer than we think. But a world where God has gone silent, where no truth is being spoken, where no prophetic voice challenges the way things are, that is a world starving to death and not even knowing it. The famine of hearing God's word is the judgment Amos feared most.

Fourth, judgment is never God's final word. The book of Amos could have ended at the fifth vision. It would have been consistent with everything that came before. But God chose to end with a promise. He always does. Beyond the exile, beyond the collapse, beyond the silence, there is a garden. There is a homecoming. There is a God who plants.

TALKING POINTS

1. **Amos prayed for mercy after the first two visions, but he was silent after the third.** What do you think changed? Is there a point where even prayer can't stop the consequences of sin? How does that shape the way you think about repentance?

2. **Amaziah told Amos to stop preaching and go home. Amos refused because God had sent him.** Have you ever been in a situation where doing the right thing meant going against someone in authority? What gave you the courage to do it, or what held you back?

3. **The merchants couldn't wait for the Sabbath to end so they could go back to cheating people.** What does it say about someone's heart when worship feels like an interruption to what they really want to do? How can you tell whether your own worship is genuine?

4. God warned of "a famine of hearing the words of the Lord." What would it look like if God went silent in your life? How does that warning change the way you value the Bible, prayer, and the people who speak truth into your life?

5. The book ends with a vision of incredible abundance and the promise that God will plant his people and never uproot them again. After everything Amos described, why do you think God chose to end with hope? What does that tell you about his character?

The book of Amos opened with a lion's roar and closed with a gardener's promise. Between those two images lay an unflinching portrait of a society that had abandoned justice and a God who refused to let injustice have the last word. The farmer from Tekoa delivered his message and, so far as we know, went home. But his words never stopped working. They are still working now.

Next, we turn to the shortest book in the Old Testament: a single chapter, a single message, aimed at a single nation. The prophet Obadiah has something to say to Edom, and it will not be pleasant.

Turn the page.

8

WHEN YOUR BROTHER TURNS HIS BACK

One of the best things about *The Super Mario Bros. Movie* is what drives the whole story: a brother who won't give up. When Mario and Luigi get separated and Luigi is captured by Bowser, Mario doesn't hesitate. He crosses kingdoms, fights enemies twice his size, and risks his life over and over again, all to get his brother back. It doesn't matter how dangerous it gets. It doesn't matter that the odds are impossible. Luigi is his brother, and brothers don't leave each other behind.

Now imagine the opposite.

Imagine that when Luigi was captured, Mario shrugged. Imagine he stood there and watched it happen. Imagine he looked on while Bowser's army dragged his brother away, and instead of running to help, he walked over and started going through Luigi's pockets. Imagine he high-fived Bowser's troops on the way out.

That's not a movie anyone would want to watch. But it's exactly what the book of Obadiah describes. A brother nation watched while its family was destroyed, did nothing to help, and then looted the wreckage. The book is only twenty-one verses long, the shortest in the entire Old Testament, but its message hits with the force of something ten times its size.

BROTHERS FROM THE BEGINNING

To understand Obadiah, you need to go all the way back to Genesis. The nation of Israel descended from a man named Jacob. The nation of Edom descended from Jacob's twin brother, Esau. From the very beginning, the relationship between these two was complicated. Jacob tricked Esau out of his birthright and his father's blessing. Esau burned with resentment. But over time, the two brothers reconciled, at least on the surface.

Their descendants were not so gracious. Israel and Edom lived as neighbors for centuries, with Edom occupying the rugged, mountainous territory southeast of the Dead Sea, in what is now southern Jordan. The relationship swung back and forth between uneasy peace and open hostility. But the family bond was always there. The law of Moses specifically told the Israelites, "Do not despise an Edomite, for the Edomites are your relatives."

That makes what happened next so much worse.

A NATION BUILT ON ROCK

Edom's geography shaped its identity. The land was dominated by towering sandstone ridges that rose over five thousand feet above sea level, riddled with narrow passes, caves, and clefts where a handful of soldiers could hold off an entire army. If you've ever seen pictures of the ancient city of Petra, carved directly into the rose-colored rock faces of southern Jordan, you've seen what Edom looked like. It was a fortress built by nature.

This geography made the Edomites proud. They looked down from their mountain strongholds and believed themselves untouchable. "Who can bring me down to the ground?" they boasted. They controlled major trade routes running north to Damascus, south toward Arabia, and west to the Mediterranean. They were wealthy, well-defended, and famous throughout the region for their wisdom. Job's friend Eliphaz came from Teman, one of Edom's key cities, and the nation had a reputation for producing shrewd advisors and skilled diplomats.

But their confidence was built on stone, not on God. And that made all the difference.

THE CRIME

The specific event that triggered Obadiah's prophecy was almost certainly the destruction of Jerusalem by the Babylonian army in 586 BC. When Nebuchadnezzar's forces besieged the city, broke through its walls, burned the temple, and marched its people into exile, it was the darkest day in Judah's history.

And Edom watched.

Worse than watched. Obadiah lays out the accusation in agonizing detail, and the sins escalate with every line. First, Edom "stood aloof" while foreigners carried off Jerusalem's wealth and cast lots to divide the plunder. They stood there and did nothing while their brother was being destroyed. That alone was a betrayal of the family bond.

But it got worse. They didn't just stand by. They gloated. They looked down on Judah "in the day of their disaster" and took pleasure in it. They opened their mouths and boasted while their relatives were being dragged away in chains.

Then they crossed the line from spectators to participants. They "marched through the gates" of Jerusalem after the Babylonians had broken them open, and they helped themselves to whatever was left. They looted the wreckage of their brother's home.

And finally, the most terrible act of all: they stationed themselves at the crossroads where refugees were fleeing the city and cut them off. They captured survivors and handed them over to the Babylonians. The people who escaped the sword were betrayed by their own family and sent back to the enemy.

Eight times in four verses, Obadiah says, "You should not have." You should not have gloated. You should not have rejoiced. You should not have entered the gates. You should not have seized their wealth. You should not have waited at the crossroads. You should not have handed over the survivors. Each accusation builds on the last, tracing a sickening arc from passive indifference to active cruelty.

PRIDE BEFORE THE FALL

God's response to Edom's betrayal fills the first half of the book and leaves no room for doubt: judgment is coming, and it will be total.

"The pride of your heart has deceived you," God says, "you who live in the clefts of the rocks and make your home on the heights, you who say to yourself, 'Who can bring me down to the ground?' Though you soar like the eagle and make your nest among the stars, from there I will bring you down."

The Edomites thought their mountains made them safe. They thought their rocky fortresses put them beyond the reach of any enemy. They were right about human enemies. But they forgot about God.

And God promises that when judgment falls, it will be thorough. If thieves break into your house, they take what they want and leave the rest. If grape pickers harvest your vineyard, they leave a few clusters behind for the poor. But what's coming to Edom will be worse than thieves and more thorough than a harvest. Everything will be taken. Their hidden treasures will be ransacked. Their famous wisdom will vanish. Their warriors will lose their nerve. Even their allies, the nations they trusted, will turn on them and drive them out of their own land.

The punishment fits the crime in every detail. Edom handed over survivors? Edom will have no survivors. Edom gloated over a brother's ruin? Shame will cover Edom forever. Edom stood by while Jerusalem was plundered? Edom will be plundered completely, with no one to stand by them.

"As you have done, it will be done to you. Your deeds will return upon your own head."

THE DAY OF THE LORD

Obadiah doesn't limit the judgment to Edom alone. He broadens the lens to include "all nations." The day of the Lord is coming, and on that day, every nation that has mistreated God's people will answer for it. This isn't tribal revenge. This is the principle that God holds all nations accountable for how they treat the vulnerable, and especially for how they treat his people.

The Edomites who drank in celebration on God's holy mountain while Jerusalem burned would find themselves staggering under a different cup entirely: the cup of God's judgment. All the nations who joined in the party would drink from that same cup until they collapsed and "were as though they had never been."

BUT ON MOUNT ZION

Then the tone shifts. After fourteen verses of condemnation, the final seven verses turn toward hope. And the hope is as specific as the judgment.

"But on Mount Zion will be deliverance; it will be holy, and Jacob will possess his inheritance."

God promises that the exiles will return. The land that was taken will be reclaimed. The territories lost to Edom, to the Philistines, to every encroaching neighbor will be restored. People will come back from as far away as Zarephath in the north, on the coast near Sidon, and from Sepharad, possibly as distant as Sardis in modern Turkey. No matter how far they've been scattered, God will bring them home.

The geographical details paint a picture of total restoration. The Negev in the south will reclaim Edom's mountains. The western foothills will expand into Philistine territory. The land of Ephraim and Samaria, lost when the northern kingdom fell to Assyria, will be repossessed. Benjamin will take back Gilead across the Jordan. Every piece of the promised land that had been chipped away by enemies and exile will be gathered back together.

And the final line of the book delivers the message that holds everything together: "The kingdom will be the Lord's."

Not Edom's. Not Babylon's. Not any human empire's. The kingdom belongs to God. He is the one who judges, and he is the one who restores. Human nations rise and fall, but the God who made a promise to Abraham, who brought Israel out of Egypt, who survived the destruction of his own temple, that God still reigns. And his kingdom has no end.

WHAT THIS MEANS FOR US

First, family loyalty is sacred to God. Edom's sin wasn't just political. It was personal. They betrayed a brother. God takes the bonds between people seriously, whether those bonds are biological, covenantal, or simply the shared humanity that connects us all. When someone who should have your back stabs you instead, God notices. And he cares.

Second, doing nothing is not the same as being innocent. Edom's first sin was standing aloof. They didn't attack Jerusalem themselves, at least not at first. They just watched. But in God's eyes, watching your brother suffer when you could have helped is a sin all by itself. Neutrality in the face of injustice isn't neutral. It's a choice, and it's the wrong one.

Third, pride is a setup for a fall. The Edomites' confidence was built on geography, not on God. They looked at their rocky fortresses and asked, "Who can bring me down?" The answer was always the same: the God they ignored. Any time we build our security on something other than God, whether it's money, reputation, strength, or position, we're making the same mistake Edom made.

Fourth, God's justice eventually balances the books. "As you have done, it will be done to you." That principle doesn't always play out on our timetable. Obadiah may not have lived to see Edom's fall. But God's justice is real, even when it's slow.

The wrongs that seem to go unpunished don't go unseen. And the day is coming when every account will be settled.

TALKING POINTS

1. **Edom and Israel were related through Esau and Jacob.** How does a family connection make betrayal worse than if it came from a stranger? Have you ever been let down by someone who was supposed to be on your side? How did it feel?

2. **Edom's first sin was standing by and doing nothing while Jerusalem was attacked.** Why is doing nothing in the face of someone else's suffering considered a sin? Can you think of situations in your life where staying silent or standing back would be wrong?

3. **The Edomites believed their mountain strongholds made them invincible.** What are some things people today put their confidence in instead of God? What happens when those things fail?

4. **"As you have done, it will be done to you."** Do you think this principle is always true? How does believing in God's justice change the way you handle situations where someone wrongs you and seems to get away with it?

5. **The book ends with "The kingdom will be the Lord's."** Why is that the right ending for a book about betrayal, judgment, and restoration? What does it mean for you to believe that God's kingdom will outlast every human empire and every human wrong?

The shortest book in the Old Testament is finished. But the biggest story in the Minor Prophets is about to begin. A prophet receives a mission from God, and instead of obeying, he runs the other direction. What happens next involves a storm, a giant fish, a city on the brink of destruction, and a question God never quite answers.

Turn the page.

9

RUNNING FROM GOD

Mark Twain's *Adventures of Huckleberry Finn* opens with a boy who wants out. Huck has been taken in by the Widow Douglas, who's trying to civilize him, make him wear clean clothes, go to school, and sit still in church. Huck hates all of it. So he does what any self-respecting runaway would do: he fakes his own death, builds a raft, and floats down the Mississippi River, heading as far from responsibility as the current will carry him.

The thing is, running doesn't work. The further Huck goes down the river, the more he runs into the very things he was trying to escape: moral choices, dangerous people, and questions about right and wrong that he can't avoid no matter how many miles he puts between himself and home. The river carries him away, but it also carries him deeper into the problems he was trying to leave behind.

The prophet Jonah had the same idea and the same result. God told him to go east. He went west. God told him to preach to a city. He boarded a boat heading for the edge of the known world. And every step of his flight took him further down, deeper into trouble, and closer to the one thing he couldn't outrun: the God who sent him.

THE CALL AND THE RUN

Jonah son of Amittai was a real prophet. We know from 2 Kings 14:25 that he came from a town called Gath Hepher, in the northern kingdom of Israel, near the region of Galilee. He prophesied during the reign of King Jeroboam II, around the middle of the eighth century BC, the same era as Amos and Hosea. He had predicted that Israel would expand its borders, and it happened. He was an established voice, a credible prophet with a track record.

Then God gave him an assignment that changed everything.

"Go to the great city of Nineveh and preach against it, because its wickedness has come up before me."

Nineveh was the major city of Assyria, located on the Tigris River about five hundred miles northeast of Israel, roughly a month's journey on foot. In Jonah's time, Assyria wasn't yet the unstoppable superpower it would later become, but the Assyrians had a long and bloody history with Israel. They were famous for their cruelty in war. Within a few decades, Assyria would conquer the northern kingdom, destroy Samaria, and deport tens of thousands of Israelites. Jonah may have already suspected this was coming, especially if he had heard Hosea's warnings about a coming Assyrian threat.

So when God said, "Go to Nineveh," Jonah heard something deeper. He knew God's character. He knew that if the Ninevites heard the warning and repented, God would forgive them. And if God forgave the Assyrians, that meant the very nation destined to destroy Israel would survive. Jonah didn't want to be the prophet who saved his people's future executioner.

His response was immediate and absolute. "But Jonah ran away from the Lord and headed for Tarshish."

Tarshish was probably located in southern Spain or the western Mediterranean, as far from Nineveh as a person could physically travel in the ancient world. Jonah went down to the port of Joppa on the Mediterranean coast, found a ship sailing west, paid the fare, and climbed aboard. The text says he was fleeing "from the Lord's presence," as if putting an ocean between himself and God would somehow break the connection.

And notice the direction. The text says Jonah went "down" to Joppa. He went "down" into the ship. He went "down" below deck. Every step away from God is a step downward, and Jonah is sinking before he ever hits the water.

THE STORM

God's response to Jonah's flight was swift and dramatic. He hurled a violent wind at the sea. The Hebrew word for "hurled" is the same word used later when the sailors hurl the cargo overboard and eventually hurl Jonah himself into the waves. God threw the storm at the ocean the way you'd throw a ball at a wall.

The ship was in serious trouble. The experienced sailors, men who had spent their lives on the water, were terrified. Each one cried out to his own god, because in the ancient world, sailors from different countries carried different beliefs. They threw the cargo overboard to lighten the ship, doing everything they knew how to do to survive.

And Jonah? Jonah was asleep.

While a dozen men fought for their lives above deck, the prophet of God was unconscious in the hold. The captain found him and was furious. "How can you sleep? Get up and call on your god! Maybe he will take notice of us, and we won't perish." A pagan sea captain had to wake up a prophet of the living God and tell him to pray. The irony is thick enough to choke on.

When prayer and physical effort both failed, the sailors cast lots to determine who had brought this disaster on them. The lot fell on Jonah. They peppered him with questions: Who are you? Where do you come from? What have you done?

Jonah answered, "I am a Hebrew, and I worship the Lord, the God of heaven, who made the sea and the dry land."

The sailors were terrified. They knew now that they weren't dealing with a minor local deity. The God who made the sea was the one sending the storm. And the man responsible for angering him was standing right in front of them.

MAN OVERBOARD

"What should we do to you to make the sea calm down for us?" the sailors asked.

Jonah's answer was stunning: "Pick me up and throw me into the sea, and it will become calm. I know that it is my fault that this great storm has come upon you."

There are two ways to read this moment. On one hand, Jonah is finally accepting responsibility for what he's done. His disobedience put these men in danger, and he's willing to pay the price. On the other hand, Jonah would rather die than go to Nineveh. He's choosing the ocean over obedience.

What happens next reveals the character of these pagan sailors in a light that shames the prophet. They didn't throw Jonah overboard. Not yet. Instead, "the men did their best to row back to land." They tried to save him. These rough, polytheistic sailors showed more compassion for Jonah than Jonah had been willing to show for the entire city of Nineveh.

But the storm only intensified. Finally, with no other option, the sailors cried out to the Lord: "Please, Lord, do not let us die for taking this man's life. Do not hold us accountable for killing an innocent man, for you, Lord, have done as you pleased." Even in the act of throwing Jonah overboard, they prayed for forgiveness. They recognized God's sovereignty. They respected human life. They acted with more reverence than the prophet himself had shown.

They threw Jonah in. The sea went still.

And then something remarkable happened. "The men greatly feared the Lord, and they offered a sacrifice to the Lord and made vows to him." These pagan sailors, who had started the voyage crying out to their various gods, ended it worshiping the God of Israel. Jonah's rebellion, meant to prevent Gentiles from encountering God, had led directly to a group of Gentiles encountering God. Even when Jonah refused to be a missionary, God used him as one.

THE FISH

"Now the Lord provided a huge fish to swallow Jonah, and Jonah was inside the fish three days and three nights."

The text doesn't name the species. It doesn't explain the biology. It simply says God "provided" a great fish, the same word used later when God provides a plant, a worm, and a scorching wind. Everything in this story is under God's direct control. The fish isn't a punishment. It's a rescue. Without it, Jonah would have drowned.

Three days and three nights in the belly of a fish. It's the detail that everybody remembers about Jonah, and it's the detail Jesus himself pointed to as a sign of his own death and resurrection. "For as Jonah was three days and three nights in the belly of a huge fish," Jesus said, "so the Son of Man will be three days and three nights in the heart of the earth" (Matthew 12:40). What happened to Jonah in the depths of the Mediterranean became a preview of what would happen to Jesus in the depths of the tomb. Both went down into darkness. Both came back.

THE PRAYER FROM THE DEEP

Chapter 2 contains Jonah's prayer from inside the fish. It reads like a psalm, drawing on the language and imagery of Israel's worship songs. And it's not a prayer of repentance, exactly. It's a prayer of thanksgiving. Jonah isn't apologizing for running. He's thanking God for not letting him drown.

"From deep in the realm of the dead I called for help, and you listened to my cry." Jonah describes his descent in terrifying detail. God hurled him into the deep. The currents swirled around him. The waves crashed over his head. Seaweed wrapped around him as he sank to the roots of the mountains, to the very floor of the ocean. He felt the gates of death closing behind him, bars locking him into the underworld forever.

"But you, Lord my God, brought my life up from the pit." At the last possible moment, when the darkness was total and the way back seemed permanently sealed, God pulled him out. Not all the way out. Not back to dry land. But out of death and into the belly of a fish, which, compared to drowning, was a significant upgrade.

The prayer ends with a line that serves as the turning point of the entire book: "Salvation comes from the Lord."

It's a beautiful statement. It's also deeply ironic, because Jonah believes this truth about himself but refuses to believe it about the Ninevites. He's grateful that God saved him from the consequences of his disobedience. He is not at all interested in God saving the Assyrians from the consequences of theirs. Salvation comes from the Lord, as long as it's coming to Jonah.

The fish vomited Jonah onto dry land. After three days in the dark, the prophet is back on solid ground, blinking in the sunlight, smelling like the inside of a sea creature, and facing the same God who called him in the first place.

The running is over. But the story is far from finished.

WHAT THIS MEANS FOR US

First, you can't outrun God. Jonah tried. He booked passage on a ship heading in the opposite direction from where God told him to go. He went down and down and down, as far from God's assignment as geography would allow. And God was waiting at every stop. You cannot put enough distance between yourself and God to escape his reach. The psalm says it best: "Where can I go from your Spirit? Where can I flee from your presence?" The answer is nowhere.

Second, disobedience doesn't just affect you. Jonah's flight endangered an entire ship full of innocent people. When we run from what God has called us to do, the fallout doesn't stay contained. It spills over onto the people around us: friends, family, classmates, teammates. Our choices have consequences beyond ourselves, and ignoring a calling from God is never a private decision.

Third, God uses imperfect people despite themselves. The sailors came to worship God because of Jonah's failure, not his faithfulness. Even Jonah's rebellion became an occasion for God to reveal himself to people who didn't know him. That doesn't make disobedience a good idea. But it does show that God's purposes are bigger than our mistakes. He can work through a reluctant prophet, a terrified crew, and even the belly of a fish.

Fourth, rock bottom can be the starting point of rescue. Jonah had to sink all the way to the ocean floor before he looked up. Sometimes we have to go all the way down before we're ready to let God bring us back up. If you feel like you're at the lowest point you've ever been, you might be exactly where Jonah was: at the place where the only direction left is up, and the only voice left to call on is God's.

TALKING POINTS

1. **When God told Jonah to go to Nineveh, Jonah ran the other way.** Have you ever known what God (or your conscience) was telling you to do and deliberately avoided it? What happened?

2. **The pagan sailors showed more compassion for Jonah than Jonah showed for the Ninevites.** What does it say when people who don't know God act more kindly than people who

do? Have you ever been surprised by kindness from an unexpected person?

3. **Jonah would rather die than go to Nineveh. Some scholars think he was trying to protect Israel from Assyria by preventing the Ninevites from repenting.** Does that change how you see his rebellion? Can doing the wrong thing ever be motivated by love for the right people?

4. **Jonah's prayer in the fish is full of thanksgiving but contains no apology.** Why do you think that is? Is it possible to be grateful for God's rescue and still not fully surrender to his plan? Have you ever experienced something like that?

5. **"Salvation comes from the Lord." Jonah said this about himself but didn't want it to be true for the Ninevites.** Why is it so hard to accept that God's grace extends to people we think don't deserve it? Who in your life do you struggle to believe God could love as much as he loves you?

Jonah is back on dry land, but his journey is only half finished. In the next chapter, he'll finally go to Nineveh, and what happens there will challenge everything he thought he knew about the God he serves. The most reluctant missionary in history is about to witness the most dramatic repentance in the Bible, and he won't be happy about it.

Turn the page.

10

THE QUESTION GOD NEVER ANSWERS

Everybody in class saw it happen. The kid who had been mean to people all year, the one who cut in line and copied homework and made fun of anyone who was different, finally got caught. The teacher called them up front. The whole room went quiet. This was going to be good. Justice was finally going to land on the person who deserved it most.

And then the teacher said, "I forgive you. Sit down."

That's it? No detention? No phone call home? No consequences? You sat there staring at your desk, and something hot and tight rose in your chest. It wasn't sadness. It wasn't confusion. It was anger. Because you knew that if it had been you, there would have been consequences. And now the worst person in the class just walked away free, and you were supposed to be okay with that.

That feeling, the fury that erupts when someone you think deserves punishment gets mercy instead, is exactly what drives the second half of the book of Jonah. The reluctant prophet finally obeys God, goes to Nineveh, preaches a five-word sermon, watches an entire city repent, and then sits down outside the walls and wishes he were dead. Not because the mission failed. Because it worked.

THE SECOND CALL

After three days in the belly of a fish and an inglorious arrival on a beach somewhere along the Mediterranean coast, Jonah received the same call he'd received before. "Go to the great city of Nineveh and proclaim to it the message I give you."

Same city. Same command. God doesn't revise his instructions just because you ignored them the first time. But notice what's different: God doesn't scold Jonah. He doesn't lecture him about his disobedience. He doesn't bring up the storm, the sailors, or the fish. He simply repeats the call and gives Jonah a second chance. That's grace. Quiet, unremarkable, completely undeserved grace.

This time, Jonah obeyed. He made the long journey northeast, roughly five hundred miles across open terrain, a trip that would have taken about a month on foot. When he finally reached the outskirts of Nineveh, the scale of the city must have been staggering. The text says it took three days to go through it. Whether that refers to the walled city itself or to the greater metropolitan area that included surrounding towns like Calah and Resen, the point is clear: Nineveh was enormous. It was one of the largest urban centers in the ancient world, teeming with people who worshiped gods that were not the God of Israel.

Jonah walked into the city and began to preach. His message was exactly five words long in the original language: "Forty more days and Nineveh will be overthrown."

That's it. No explanation. No call to repentance. No instructions about what the Ninevites should do. No offer of mercy. Just a countdown to destruction. Jonah delivered the bare minimum. He was obedient in his feet but not in his heart.

A CITY ON ITS KNEES

What happened next is one of the most astonishing things in the entire Bible. The Ninevites believed God.

Not after weeks of preaching. Not after signs and wonders. Not after a long theological debate. Immediately. From the greatest to the least, the people of Nineveh declared a fast and put on sackcloth, the rough, uncomfortable garment that symbolized mourning and repentance in the ancient world.

When word reached the king, he rose from his throne, took off his royal robes, covered himself with sackcloth, and sat down in ashes. Then he issued an official decree that went further than anything Jonah had asked for. No person or animal was to eat or drink anything. Every human and every beast was to be covered in sackcloth. Everyone was to cry out urgently to God and give up their evil ways and their violence.

The decree ended with a line that captures the heart of the entire scene: "Who knows? God may yet relent and with compassion turn from his fierce anger so that we will not perish."

"Who knows?" Those two words reveal something important about the Ninevites' repentance. They weren't bargaining with God. They weren't treating repentance as a transaction: we'll fast, and you'll forgive. They were throwing themselves on the mercy of a God they barely understood, with no guarantee that it would work. They repented because it was the right thing to do, not because they were promised a reward. And somehow, in that honest, humble uncertainty, they stumbled onto the very thing that moves the heart of God.

"When God saw what they did, how they turned from their evil ways, he relented and did not bring on them the destruction he had threatened."

The countdown stopped. Nineveh was spared.

THE ANGRIEST PROPHET IN THE BIBLE

You might expect the next verse to say, "And Jonah rejoiced." It doesn't.

"But to Jonah this seemed very wrong, and he became angry."

Not disappointed. Not conflicted. Angry. The original language is even stronger: it could be translated as Jonah perceived this as a great evil. The salvation of 120,000 people struck Jonah as a catastrophe.

And then, in one of the most revealing prayers in Scripture, Jonah tells God exactly why he ran in the first place. "Isn't this what I said, Lord, when I was still at home? That is what I tried to forestall by fleeing to Tarshish. I knew that you are a gracious and compassionate God, slow to anger and abounding in love, a God who relents from sending calamity."

There it is. The reason behind the flight, the storm, the fish, all of it. Jonah didn't run because he was afraid of Nineveh. He ran because he was afraid God would do exactly what God did: forgive them. Jonah knew God's character. He could quote the ancient description of God that Moses received at Mount Sinai: gracious, compassionate, slow to anger, abounding in love. And he hated it. Not because it applied to him, of course. Jonah was perfectly happy to be on the receiving end of God's mercy when he was drowning in the Mediterranean. He just didn't want the same mercy extended to the people who might one day destroy his country.

This is the dark heart of the book. Jonah didn't have a theology problem. He had a mercy problem. He believed everything true about God. He just didn't want those truths to apply to his enemies.

"Now, Lord, take away my life," Jonah said, "for it is better for me to die than to live."

The man who almost drowned running from God now wants to die because God was too kind. And God's response is a single, devastating question: "Is it right for you to be angry?"

Jonah doesn't answer. He walks out of the city, builds himself a shelter, sits down, and waits. Maybe he's hoping Nineveh will sin again and God will change his mind. Maybe he's sulking. Either way, he's not finished being angry.

THE PLANT, THE WORM, AND THE WIND

What follows is one of the strangest and most beautiful object lessons in the Bible.

God provided a leafy plant that grew up overnight and spread its leaves over Jonah's head, giving him shade from the brutal sun. Jonah was thrilled. The text says he was "very happy" about the plant, using the same intense language that described his anger a few verses earlier. Jonah, who couldn't find it in himself to be happy about the salvation of an entire city, was overjoyed about a vine.

Then, at dawn the next day, God provided a worm. The worm attacked the plant, and it withered. Then God provided a scorching east wind, and the sun blazed down on Jonah's head until he grew faint. Once again, he wanted to die. "It would be better for me to die than to live."

God asked the question a second time: "Is it right for you to be angry about the plant?"

"It is," Jonah snapped. "And I'm angry enough to die."

Now God delivers the lesson, and it arrives not as a lecture but as a question.

"You have been concerned about this plant, though you did not tend it or make it grow. It sprang up overnight and died overnight. And should I not have concern for the great city of Nineveh, in which there are more than a hundred and twenty thousand people who cannot tell their right hand from their left, and also many animals?"

The logic is inescapable. Jonah grieved over a plant he didn't create, didn't water, and didn't grow. It existed for one day. He invested nothing in it. And yet its loss filled him with enough anguish to wish for death. How much more, then, should God grieve over a city full of human beings he created, people so confused they couldn't tell right from wrong, people whose lives mattered infinitely more than a vine?

And the book ends there. Right there. With a question hanging in the air, unanswered.

THE QUESTION THAT'S MEANT FOR YOU

Most books in the Bible end with a statement. Jonah ends with a question. God asks, "Should I not have concern for the great city of Nineveh?" and no one responds. Jonah doesn't answer. The narrator doesn't answer. The silence is deliberate, because the question isn't really for Jonah anymore. It's for the reader. It's for you.

Should God have concern for people you consider enemies? Should his mercy extend to people who have done terrible things? Should the same grace that rescued you from your worst moments also rescue the people you'd rather see punished?

The entire book has been building toward this moment. The sailors in chapter 1 showed more compassion than Jonah. The Ninevites in chapter 3 repented more sincerely than Israel ever did. And Jonah, the prophet of the living God, cared more about a plant than about 120,000 human beings. The story holds up a mirror, and the reflection isn't flattering. We are all more like Jonah than we want to admit. We love mercy when it's aimed at us. We resist it when it's aimed at people we think don't deserve it.

But "salvation comes from the Lord," as Jonah himself said from inside the fish. And if salvation comes from God, then God gets to decide who receives it. Not Jonah. Not us. God.

WHAT THIS MEANS FOR US

First, God gives second chances. Jonah failed spectacularly. He ran, he hid, he nearly died. And God called him again with the same mission, no strings attached. If God can give Jonah a second chance after that level of rebellion, he can give you a second chance too. Your past failures don't disqualify you from God's purposes.

Second, genuine repentance doesn't demand guarantees. The Ninevites said, "Who knows? God may yet relent." They didn't repent because they were promised forgiveness. They repented because they recognized that their lives were wrong and that a holy God had every right to judge them. Real repentance doesn't negotiate. It surrenders.

Third, the mercy you want for yourself is the same mercy God offers to others. Jonah wanted grace for himself and judgment for Nineveh. God pointed out the contradiction. You can't celebrate mercy when it saves you and resent it when it saves someone else. Grace is either for everyone or it isn't grace at all.

Fourth, God's compassion extends further than we're comfortable with. The book of Jonah doesn't just say that God is merciful. It shows that God's mercy reaches people we would never choose to forgive: enemies, outsiders, entire cities full of people who don't know him. If that makes you uncomfortable, you're in good company. It made Jonah uncomfortable too. But discomfort with God's mercy is not a sign that something is wrong with God. It's a sign that something needs to change in us.

TALKING POINTS

1. **Jonah preached the shortest and least enthusiastic sermon in the Bible, and the entire city repented.** What does this say about God's ability to work through imperfect messengers? Have you ever seen something good happen despite someone's bad attitude or half-hearted effort?

2. **The Ninevites said, "Who knows? God may yet relent."** Why is that kind of humble uncertainty actually a sign

of genuine faith? How is it different from trying to bargain with God?

3. **Jonah was angrier about a dead plant than about the potential destruction of 120,000 people.** What does that reveal about how our emotions can get attached to the wrong things? Have you ever been more upset about something small and personal than about something big and important?

4. **The book ends with a question, not an answer.** Why do you think the author chose to end it that way? How would you answer God's question: "Should I not have concern for the great city of Nineveh?"

5. **Jonah wanted mercy for himself but judgment for his enemies.** Be honest: is there anyone in your life you'd rather see punished than forgiven? What would it look like to let God's compassion reshape how you feel about that person?

The story of Jonah is finished, but its final question lingers. It lingered for its first readers, it lingered for Jesus when he pointed to Jonah as a sign of something greater, and it lingers for us. The God who chases reluctant prophets, calms storms, commands fish, grows plants, and sends worms is the same God who looks at a city full of lost people and says, "Should I not have concern?"

The answer, whether Jonah ever admitted it or not, is yes.

Now we turn to the last prophet in this volume: Micah, a man from a small town with a big message about justice, mercy, and the coming of a king from the most unlikely of places.

Turn the page.

11

THE SHEPHERD WHO WOULDN'T BE QUIET

Bram Stoker's *Dracula* is terrifying for a lot of reasons, but the deepest horror in the story isn't the fangs or the coffin or the creepy castle in Transylvania. It's the idea that someone in a position of power and trust is secretly feeding on the very people he's supposed to protect. Count Dracula presents himself as a nobleman. He's wealthy, educated, and charming. But behind the polished exterior, he survives by draining the life out of ordinary people. The more he takes from them, the stronger he gets. The weaker they become, the less they can fight back.

The prophet Micah described the leaders of Israel in almost the same terms. Not vampires, exactly, but something just as disturbing. He accused the rulers and judges of his nation of tearing the skin off God's people, stripping the flesh from their bones, breaking their bones apart, and chopping the people up "like meat in a pot." It's one of the most graphic images in the entire Bible, and Micah used it to describe not foreign enemies but Israel's own leaders. The people in charge of justice were devouring the people they were supposed to serve.

Micah was a small-town prophet with a big-city message, and he delivered it with the kind of courage that only comes from knowing you've been sent by God.

A VOICE FROM THE COUNTRY

Micah came from Moresheth Gath, a village in the Shephelah, the rolling foothills between the Mediterranean coast and the mountains of Judah. It was about twenty miles southwest of Jerusalem, surrounded by farmland, vineyards, and fortified towns that guarded the approaches to the capital. Micah wasn't a city prophet. He wasn't part of the religious establishment in Jerusalem or the political machinery in Samaria. He was a rural outsider, and he saw things that insiders had stopped noticing.

His name means "Who is like the Lord?" and the book that bears his name circles back to that question in its very last chapter: "Who is a God like you?" His ministry stretched across the reigns of three kings of Judah: Jotham, Ahaz, and Hezekiah, spanning roughly the second half of the eighth century BC, from about 750–686. He was a contemporary of Isaiah in Jerusalem and Hosea in the north, but his perspective was different from both. Micah spoke from the ground level, from the villages where ordinary people felt the weight of unjust policies made by powerful people far away.

What drove Micah wasn't professional training or political ambition. It was the Spirit of God. "I am filled with power, with the Spirit of the Lord, and with justice and might to declare to Jacob his transgression, to Israel his sin." That single sentence tells you everything you need to know about this prophet. He had power, not from wealth or position but from God. He had justice, not the kind that could be bought but the kind that burned. And he had a message that the people in charge did not want to hear.

GOD COMES DOWN

The book opens with a courtroom scene that stretches across the entire earth. "Hear, you peoples, all of you. Listen, earth and all who live in it. The Sovereign Lord is about to take the witness stand."

God is coming out of his holy temple. He is stepping down from heaven to the high places of the earth. When his feet touch the mountains, they melt like wax before a fire. The valleys split open. It's the language of an earthquake and a volcano rolled into one, and it describes what happens when the God of justice shows up to confront a nation that has abandoned him.

The reason for this terrifying appearance? "All this is because of Jacob's transgression, because of the sins of Israel. What is Jacob's transgression? Is it not Samaria? What is Judah's high place? Is it not Jerusalem?"

Both capitals are named. Both kingdoms are guilty. Samaria in the north has filled itself with idolatry, and Jerusalem in the south is following the same path. Micah doesn't play favorites. His own country, Judah, is no better than the northern kingdom everyone loved to criticize.

The sentence on Samaria is devastating. God will turn the city into a heap of rubble and pour its stones into the valley below. The great city built by King Omri on a hill three hundred feet high will be dismantled stone by stone. This prophecy was fulfilled in 722 BC when the Assyrians conquered Samaria and deported its people. You can still see the scattered stones today.

A LAMENT FOR HOME

But Micah's grief hits closest to home when he turns to the towns of the Shephelah, his own backyard. In a passage packed with wordplays on the names of local villages, he describes the advance of the Assyrian army through western Judah. Each town name becomes a bitter pun on its fate.

"Tell it not in Gath," he says, echoing David's ancient lament for Saul. "In Beth Ophrah, roll in the dust." Ophrah sounds like the word for "dust." "Pass by, inhabitants of Shaphir." Shaphir means "pleasant," but there is nothing pleasant about exile. The wordplays continue town by town, tracing a path of destruction through the very villages where Micah grew up, where he knew the farmers and the families and the children.

This isn't abstract prophecy. Micah is watching his neighbors lose everything. In 701 BC, the Assyrian king Sennacherib invaded Judah and systematically destroyed the fortified towns of the Shephelah. His own records boast of conquering forty-six of Hezekiah's strong cities. The famous reliefs from Sennacherib's palace in Nineveh depict the siege of Lachish, the most important fortress in Micah's region, in brutal detail: siege ramps, battering rams, soldiers impaled on stakes, families marched away in chains.

Micah saw this coming. He mourned it before it happened, walking barefoot and stripped like a prisoner of war, wailing like a jackal, moaning like an owl. The prophet didn't just announce judgment. He felt it.

THE MIDNIGHT PLOTTERS

Chapter 2 zeroes in on the specific crime that is rotting Israel from the inside. It's not idolatry this time, though that's part of the picture. It's economic exploitation, and Micah describes it with chilling precision.

"Woe to those who plan iniquity, to those who plot evil on their beds! At morning's light they carry it out because it is in their power to do it."

These are men who lie awake at night scheming about how to take what belongs to someone else. When the sun comes up, they execute their plans. They covet fields and seize them. They covet houses and take them. They defraud people of their homes and strip families of their inheritance.

In ancient Israel, land was sacred. It wasn't just property. It was a family's identity, their connection to the promises God made when he brought them into the land. The law of Moses included protections to make sure land stayed in families permanently. But the wealthy and powerful had found ways around the law. They manipulated the courts. They lent money at impossible rates. When families couldn't pay, they seized the land. The rich got richer. The poor lost everything. And the legal system that was supposed to prevent this was the very tool being used to carry it out.

God's response matches the crime perfectly. "I am planning disaster against this people," he says, using the same word for "planning" that was used to describe the plotters in their beds. They plotted evil against the helpless. God is plotting judgment against them. And when it comes, there will be no one left in the "assembly of the Lord" to divide the land they stole.

PROPHETS PEOPLE WANT TO HEAR

The powerful don't just steal land. They also silence anyone who objects. "Do not prophesy," they tell Micah and prophets like him. "Do not prophesy about these things. Disgrace will not overtake us."

The people preferred prophets who told them what they wanted to hear. Micah puts it with devastating sarcasm: "If a liar and deceiver comes and says, 'I will prophesy for you plenty of wine and beer,' that would be just the prophet for this people!" Give us a preacher who talks about comfort and prosperity, not one who talks about justice and accountability. That's the kind of prophet Israel wanted.

But Micah refused to be that kind of prophet. And his refusal sets up the most dramatic contrast in these chapters.

SHEPHERDS TURNED CANNIBALS

Chapter 3 contains the fiercest indictment of corrupt leadership in the prophetic books. Micah addresses the rulers directly: "Should you not know justice, you who hate good and love evil?"

Then comes the cannibal metaphor, extended and grotesque on purpose. "You tear the skin from my people and the flesh from their bones. You eat my people's flesh, strip off their skin, break their bones in pieces, and chop them up like meat for the pan, like flesh for the pot."

This is what it looks like when leaders use their power to consume the people they govern. The imagery is sickening because the reality is sickening. These rulers were supposed to be shepherds. Instead, they were butchers. And when disaster finally comes and they cry out to God for help, he will not answer. They turned a deaf ear to the cries of the oppressed. God will turn a deaf ear to theirs.

The false prophets come next. They prophesy peace for anyone who feeds them and declare war against anyone who doesn't put food in their mouths. They are prophets for hire, adjusting their message to match the size of the payment. God's judgment on them is fitting: darkness. They will receive no more visions. They will have no answers. They will cover their faces in shame because there is no word from God.

Against this backdrop of corruption, Micah makes his own declaration: "But as for me, I am filled with power, with the Spirit of the Lord, and with justice and might, to declare to Jacob his transgression, to Israel his sin." While the false prophets preach whatever pays, Micah preaches what's true. While the rulers devour the people, Micah stands with them. He has no institution behind him, no royal backing, no wealthy patrons. He has the Spirit of God. And that is enough.

THE UNTHINKABLE SENTENCE

The chapter ends with a sentence so shocking that it was remembered for more than a century. Micah accuses the leaders of building Zion with bloodshed and Jerusalem with wickedness. The rulers judge for a bribe. The priests teach for a price. The prophets tell fortunes for money. And yet, leaning on God like a crutch, they say, "Is not the Lord among us? No disaster will come upon us."

They believed that God's presence in the temple guaranteed their safety, no matter how they behaved. Micah shattered that illusion with three lines that must have left his audience speechless.

"Therefore because of you, Zion will be plowed like a field, Jerusalem will become a heap of rubble, the temple hill a mound overgrown with thickets."

Jerusalem. The city of David. The home of the temple. Plowed like a field. It was the most radical judgment-prophecy any prophet had ever uttered. More than a hundred years later, when the prophet Jeremiah was put on trial for saying something similar, the elders saved his life by quoting this very passage from Micah. They remembered that when King Hezekiah heard Micah's words, he repented, and God relented. The prophecy worked. It changed a king's heart. And because it did, Jerusalem was spared, at least for that generation (Jeremiah 26:17–19).

WHAT THIS MEANS FOR US

First, where you come from doesn't determine what God can do through you. Micah was a nobody from a small town. He had no credentials, no connections, no platform. But he had the Spirit of God, and that gave him the authority to confront kings, priests, and prophets. God has always chosen unlikely people to carry his most important messages.

Second, leaders will be judged by how they treat the powerless. Micah's harshest words were reserved for people in authority who used their position to exploit the vulnerable. The higher the responsibility, the greater the accountability. This applies to anyone who has influence over others, whether in government, in church, in school, or in a family.

Third, comfortable lies are more popular than uncomfortable truths. The people preferred prophets who promised wine and beer. They silenced the ones who preached justice. We do the same thing whenever we avoid the truth because it makes us uncomfortable, or surround ourselves with voices that only tell us what we want to hear.

Fourth, God's presence is not a guarantee of God's protection. Israel assumed that having the temple meant having God's favor, regardless of how they lived. Micah corrected that assumption. Being close to God means nothing if your life contradicts everything God stands for. Worship without justice is not worship. It's self-deception.

TALKING POINTS

1. **Micah came from a small town and had no political power, yet God used him to confront the most powerful people in the nation.** What does this say about who God chooses to use? Have you ever felt too small or too unimportant to make a difference?

2. **The leaders of Israel were described as cannibals who devoured the people they were supposed to protect.** What does it look like today when people in authority exploit those under their care? How should Christians respond when they see this happening?

3. **The people preferred prophets who preached about wine and beer instead of justice and repentance.** Why is it so tempting to listen only to messages that make us feel good? How can you make sure you're hearing the truth, even when it's uncomfortable?

4. Micah said, "I am filled with power, with the Spirit of the Lord." What gave him the courage to stand alone against corrupt leaders? Where does your courage come from when you need to speak up for what's right?

5. The leaders said, "Is not the Lord among us? No disaster will come upon us." How can religious confidence become dangerous when it's disconnected from obedience? Can you think of examples where people use their faith as an excuse to avoid accountability?

Micah has torn down the illusions. The leaders are exposed. The prophets are silenced. Jerusalem's fate hangs in the balance. But the prophet from Moresheth isn't finished. In the chapters ahead, he will paint one of the most beautiful visions of the future in all of Scripture: swords beaten into plowshares, a ruler born in Bethlehem, and a God who asks for nothing more than justice, mercy, and a humble walk with him.

Turn the page.

12

WHAT GOD REALLY WANTS

In *Cars 2*, Mater is the last car anyone would pick for an international mission. He's a rusty tow truck from Radiator Springs, a tiny town so far off the map that most of the world doesn't know it exists. When he ends up surrounded by sleek, sophisticated cars in the world of international racing, nobody takes him seriously. He's loud, unsophisticated, and completely out of place.

But Mater turns out to be the one who saves everyone. Not in spite of being a small-town tow truck, but because of it. His honesty, his loyalty, his refusal to pretend to be something he wasn't—those are exactly what the situation required. The hero didn't come from the world stage. He came from a place nobody noticed.

The prophet Micah had something similar to say about a village called Bethlehem. It was small. It was insignificant. It barely registered on the map. And yet, Micah declared, this tiny place would produce a ruler whose kingdom would stretch to the ends of the earth. Out of the smallest and most unlikely location in all of Judah, God would bring the greatest king the world would ever know.

That's the heart of Micah 4–7. After three chapters of devastating judgment, the prophet turns a corner. The darkness doesn't disappear, but a light breaks through it: a vision of peace, a promise of a king, and one of the most famous answers to one of the most important questions in the Bible.

SWORDS INTO PLOWSHARES

The shift from chapter 3 to chapter 4 is one of the most dramatic in all of Scripture. Chapter 3 ended with Jerusalem plowed like a field and the temple hill reduced to a thicket. Chapter 4 opens with the same temple mountain lifted higher than every other peak on earth, with nations streaming toward it from every direction.

"In the last days the mountain of the Lord's temple will be established as the highest of the mountains. It will be exalted above the hills, and peoples will stream to it. Many nations will come and say, 'Come, let us go up to the mountain of the Lord, to the temple of the God of Jacob. He will teach us his ways, so that we may walk in his paths.'"

The same words appear in Isaiah 2, and whether Micah quoted Isaiah or the other way around doesn't matter. The vision belongs to God, and it's breathtaking. A world that has been defined by violence and injustice is being reimagined from the ground up. God himself will arbitrate between the nations. The disputes that used to be settled with swords will be settled with wisdom. And then comes the image that has echoed through the centuries:

"They will beat their swords into plowshares and their spears into pruning hooks. Nation will not take up sword against nation, nor will they train for war anymore."

Weapons of destruction reshaped into tools of cultivation. The metal forged to kill bent into blades that feed. And the result is the simplest, most beautiful picture of peace in the Bible: "Everyone will sit under their own vine and under their own fig tree, and no one will make them afraid."

No fear. No exploitation. No midnight plots to steal your neighbor's land. Just ordinary people living in safety, enjoying the fruit of their own labor. After everything Micah described in the first three chapters, this vision is almost too good to believe. But God stakes his own name on it: "For the Lord Almighty has spoken."

THE LAME MADE STRONG

Before the grand vision is fulfilled, there are hard days ahead. Micah doesn't skip over them. Daughter Zion will writhe in pain like a woman in labor. The people will go into exile, all the way to Babylon, a prediction that was remarkable in Micah's time since Babylon was a minor power under Assyrian control and wouldn't threaten Judah for more than a century.

But exile is not the end. "There you will be rescued. There the Lord will redeem you." The pattern Micah traces runs through all of Scripture: suffering, then deliverance. Death, then resurrection. The lame will become a remnant. The outcasts will become a strong nation. God specializes in taking what the world has discarded and turning it into something powerful.

And the nations who gathered against Jerusalem, thinking they had won, will discover that they were actually being gathered like sheaves on a threshing floor. "Rise and thresh, Daughter Zion," God commands, "for I will give you horns of iron;

I will give you hooves of bronze, and you will break to pieces many nations." The victim will become the victor, not through her own strength but through the strength God provides.

A RULER FROM BETHLEHEM

Then comes the prophecy concerning the birth of Jesus: "But you, Bethlehem Ephrathah, though you are small among the clans of Judah, out of you will come for me one who will be ruler over Israel, whose origins are from of old, from ancient times."

Bethlehem. A tiny village about five miles south of Jerusalem. The place where Rachel was buried, where Ruth met Boaz, and where a shepherd boy named David was anointed king. It was David's hometown, and by pointing back to Bethlehem, Micah was reaching past the corruption of Jerusalem's current rulers to the beginning of the royal line. The next great king wouldn't come from the halls of power. He would come from the place where the dynasty started, small and unimpressive and chosen by God alone.

Seven centuries later, when the Magi came from the east asking where the Messiah was to be born, the religious leaders in Jerusalem didn't have to search long for an answer. They quoted Micah 5:2. It was this prophecy that sent the Magi to Bethlehem, where they found a baby lying in a manger who would grow up to be the shepherd-king Micah described: one who would "stand and shepherd his flock in the strength of the Lord, in the majesty of the name of the Lord his God."

"And he will be their peace," Micah says. Not just a peacemaker. Peace itself. The one whose presence ends the conflict, whose rule makes the swords-into-plowshares vision possible, whose kingdom reaches to the ends of the earth.

WHAT HAVE I DONE TO YOU?

Chapter 6 opens with a scene that catches you off guard. After chapters of accusation and judgment, you'd expect God to be angry. Instead, he sounds hurt.

"Listen to what the Lord says: 'Stand up, plead my case before the mountains; let the hills hear what you have to say.'"

The mountains are summoned as witnesses, the oldest features of the landscape, silent observers who have watched everything from the exodus to the exile. And in front of these ancient witnesses, God doesn't thunder. He asks a question.

"My people, what have I done to you? How have I burdened you? Answer me." It's one of the most tender moments in the prophetic books. God isn't demanding an explanation. He's asking for one. What did I do wrong? When did I become such a burden that you turned away from me?

Then God recounts his own history of faithfulness. He brought them out of Egypt. He sent them Moses, Aaron, and Miriam as leaders. He turned Balaam's curse into a blessing. He carried them from Shittim to Gilgal, from the edge of the wilderness into the promised land. Every step of the way, he was there. And the only response he wanted was for them to "acknowledge the righteous acts of the Lord."

THE QUESTION AND THE ANSWER

What follows is one of the most famous exchanges in all of Scripture. An Israelite worshiper, representing the whole nation, asks the question that religion has always asked:

"With what shall I come before the Lord and bow down before the exalted God? Shall I come before him with burnt offerings, with calves a year old? Will the Lord be pleased with thousands of rams, with ten thousand rivers of olive oil? Shall I offer my firstborn for my transgression, the fruit of my body for the sin of my soul?"

Each offer escalates. A calf. Thousands of rams. Rivers of oil. And finally, the most extreme sacrifice imaginable: a first-born child. The worshiper is desperately trying to find the right price to pay for God's favor, bidding higher and higher as if God were holding an auction.

Micah's answer cuts through the escalation with a simplicity that has resonated for nearly three thousand years.

"He has shown you, O mortal, what is good. And what does the Lord require of you? To act justly and to love mercy and to walk humbly with your God."

That's it. No elaborate rituals. No impossible sacrifices. Three things. Act justly: treat people fairly, especially the powerless. Love mercy: don't just practice kindness when it's convenient, but love it, make it the reflex of your heart. Walk humbly with your God: live in step with him, not strutting ahead or lagging behind, but walking alongside him with an honest awareness of who he is and who you are.

When the Library of Congress in Washington, DC, was rebuilt in the late nineteenth century, religious leaders considered quotations from every known religious tradition to place in the alcove dedicated to religion. They chose Micah 6:8. Out of all the sacred texts in the world, this verse from a small-town prophet in ancient Judah was selected as the single best summary of what God asks from human beings.

THE DARKEST HOUR AND THE DAWN

The final chapter opens in near despair. Micah laments that the faithful have vanished. Every person hunts their neighbor with a net. The ruler demands gifts. The judge accepts bribes. You can't trust your neighbor, your friend, or even your own spouse. A man's enemies are the members of his own household.

It sounds hopeless. But then Micah plants his feet.

"But as for me, I watch in hope for the Lord, I wait for God my Savior; my God will hear me."

That single verse holds the entire book together. Between the darkness of judgment and the light of salvation stands a prophet who refuses to stop hoping. He can't see the future clearly. He doesn't know when deliverance will come. But he knows who God is, and that's enough.

WHO IS A GOD LIKE YOU?

The book closes with a passage of such beauty that it reads like a hymn. And buried in it is a wordplay that circles all the way back to the prophet's own name. "Micah" means "Who is like the Lord?" And in the final stanza, the prophet asks:

"Who is a God like you, who pardons sin and forgives the transgression of the remnant of his inheritance? You do not stay angry forever but delight to show mercy."

This is the God Micah has been pointing toward through seven chapters of accusation and promise. Not a God who enjoys punishment. A God who delights in mercy. Not a God who stays angry. A God who pardons.

And the last image in the book is unforgettable. "You will tread our sins underfoot and hurl all our iniquities into the depths of the sea." The God who hurled the Egyptians into the sea at the exodus now hurls Israel's sins into the same depths. The enemy isn't a foreign army this time. It's the sin that has separated God from his people. And God destroys it the way he destroyed Pharaoh's chariots: by drowning it where it can never be recovered.

The book ends with a reminder that all of this, the justice, the mercy, the forgiveness, the future king from Bethlehem, rests on promises God made long before Micah was born. "You will be faithful to Jacob, and show love to Abraham, as you pledged on oath to our ancestors in days long ago." The story of Israel isn't random. It's covenantal. God made promises, and God keeps them. That was true in Micah's day. It was true when Jesus was born in Bethlehem. And it's true now.

WHAT THIS MEANS FOR US

First, God's vision for the world is peace, not violence. Swords into plowshares isn't just a nice idea. It's God's stated goal for creation. Every act of peacemaking, every choice to resolve conflict without destruction, every refusal to let hatred have the last word moves the world a little closer to the future Micah described.

Second, God chooses the small and the unlikely. Bethlehem was too small to matter. Mater was too rusty to be taken seriously. Micah was too rural to be noticed. But God doesn't measure significance the way the world does. If you feel small, overlooked, or underestimated, you're in exactly the kind of position God loves to work with.

Third, what God wants from you is simpler than you think. Not thousands of rams. Not rivers of oil. Not impossible sacrifices. Justice. Mercy. Humility. Three things you can practice today, in your school, your home, your friendships, and your relationship with God.

Fourth, God delights to show mercy. That's the word Micah uses. Delights. God doesn't forgive reluctantly, like someone forced to let you off the hook. He forgives gladly, like someone who has been waiting for the chance. Your sins, hurled into the depths of the sea, are gone. That's not just good theology. That's good news.

TALKING POINTS

1. **Micah's vision of peace includes "everyone sitting under their own vine and fig tree."** What would that kind of peace look like in your life, your school, or your community? What's one step you could take toward it?

2. **The Bethlehem prophecy shows God choosing a small, insignificant place to bring about his greatest work.** Why do you think God consistently chooses the unlikely? What does this mean for people who feel like they're not enough?

3. **God asks, "My people, what have I done to you? How have I burdened you?"** What does it tell you about God's character that he asks this question instead of simply condemning? Have you ever felt like God was distant, only to realize he'd been faithful all along?

4. **"Act justly, love mercy, walk humbly with your God."** If you had to choose one of these three to focus on this week, which would it be and why? What would it look like in practice?

5. **Micah ends with God hurling sins into the depths of the sea.** What does this image mean to you personally? Is there a sin or failure you've been carrying that you need to let God throw into the deep?

We began this journey with Hosea's broken marriage and a God who refused to stop loving. We walked through Joel's locusts, Amos's roaring lion, Obadiah's betrayed brother, Jonah's storm-tossed sea, and Micah's small-town courage. Through it all, one truth has held steady: the God of the Minor Prophets is not minor. He judges because he is just. He restores because he is faithful. He forgives because he delights in mercy.

And he isn't finished yet.